PUZZLING PEOPLE:
THE LABYRINTH OF THE PSYCHOPATH

velluminous

Published by Velluminous Press
www.velluminous.com

ISBN: 978-1-905605-28-6

COVER DESIGN
HOLLY OLLIVANDER

CHAPTER START ART FEATURES
DETAILS OF ENGRAVINGS BY
PAUL GUSTAVE DORÉ

Dedicated to Victims of Psychopaths Everywhere.

It wasn't your fault.
You are not alone
and
you no longer need to suffer.

PUZZLING PEOPLE
THE LABYRINTH OF THE PSYCHOPATH

THE ONLY MISTAKES ARE THE THINGS WE DO THAT WE FAIL TO LEARN FROM

I once agreed to pick up friends from the airport. I was new in town and since I had no idea where I was going I allowed myself plenty of time to accomplish the journey. The airport was doing a lot of re-routing from construction, lots of weird turns inside the parking area, most of the signage down and so on and since I had plenty of time to spare I decided to play a little game. I thought I might picture where I wanted to be, and to imagine how it would feel to simply *know* which was the shortest route to the gate. I took left turns, right turns and detours, asking each time, *"Which way would I go if I knew where I was going?"*

I ended up next to an elevator. It felt like the right place to stop. I parked in an open spot, took the elevator up to the level that felt right and when the door opened, there I was perhaps ten feet away from the gate where my friends were due to exit the plane.

I first told this story to the author of this book, and now I am telling you. *Owning the feeling* is the same as trusting your instincts, and trusting your instincts is merely shorthand for *trusting yourself.*

Chances are, you were led to pick up this book because you've had an encounter that has changed your life. Chances are there were numerous opportunities to trust your feelings during the course of the relationship and chances are you didn't. Don't feel bad. I could tell you all about the number of times I have been lost in an airport carpark but that would probably make this book around ninety-five percent Foreword, and five percent actual book.

Red flags are our feelings telling us to pay attention. Red flags are the signage of our souls, an indication that something may be seriously out of alignment with the way we are communicating with the greater part of ourselves. We were not weak, we were not stupid, we were vulnerable, and the predator pounced. There was something in us that we felt was lacking that only this other person could ever fulfil and here's the thing: *they sniff that out*, that need we have, and then they move in for the kill.

Romantic films and love songs do us all a great disservice; the key to joy is learning that the more complete we can be in ourselves — in self-trust, self-belief and self-love — the more we attract into our lives other humans who are complete in themselves also. Then — *look out* — this is the truly magical moment when a relationship takes off and soars; two people who are together for the fun of enhancing each other's lives, not to fill some hole or missing part in each other's hearts.

THE WORD INFATUATION IS TAKEN DIRECTLY FROM THE LATIN **INFATUAT** MEANING **MADE FOOLISH**

...and maybe that's the part that really hurts the most.

It's a funny old thing, infatuation. Love expands the soul, while infatuation shrinks the intellect and debases the currency of communication. Infatuation can make you feel so high, so good. It can make you do crazy things like leap tall buildings in a single bound, then taller ones, then still taller ones. It can make you walk on burning coals or believe anything you are told. Infatuation can make you do anything short of ram a rocket up your backside and light it to achieve that lift-off again, to once more feel the wonder of the incredible illusion that someone — at long last — sees the real you and loves you, not *in spite of who you are*, but *because of who you are*. It can be the most delicious feeling in the world, until the predator, the user, the taker, the abuser moves on.

If this is where you are now, you may want to kill. You may want to die. You may want to cut your own heart out to get rid of the pain. It may feel like your thoughts are thinking you, that you are losing your mind... this is because *you are detoxing*.

You've experienced a surge of dopamine rushing through your brain stimulating a cascade of shimmering pleasure. Norepine-phrine kick-started the production of adrenaline that made your heart pound. The payoff of a phenethylamine-flooded nervous system was bliss. The primary sexual arousal hormone oxytocin mimicked the buildup of orgasm and subsequent feelings of emotional attachment. This chemical cocktail overcame critical faculties and left you defenceless to your emotional-high drug pusher.

The good news is there was never anything missing in your heart and soul, nor were you ever really lost. The moment you begin to embrace this then you will be ready to experience life *enhancement* by your own will, rather than life *diminishment* by another's ill intent.

Are you ready for the journey of your lifetime? The entire reason for this book is to show that we — the author and I — know that you are.

Holly Ollivander

HEO

WHEN THE DEMON KNOCKS AT YOUR DOOR

A psychopath coming into your life will at first seem like the beginning of an eternal springtime. They will be everything you want them to be and more. Matters not what role they choose to become in your life: lover, politician, business partner, family member, co-worker or Good Samaritan. However, their ultimate agenda is always the same: to make you declare war upon yourself, on your mind, on your soul, on the very person you are meant to be. You will be divided in order to be conquered.

From the dizzying heights of golden promises and idealism bequeathed upon you, the psychopath will systematically downgrade your psychological sovereignty by manoeuvring you into an ever-tightening spiral of self-doubt and dependency, at the end of which is the annihilation of your true being, leaving only a facsimile of what you once were. You will be exploited for your physical and emotional energy reserves in the manner of a robber raiding a gold mine until you are emptied, then abandoned.

The psychopath will then casually walk away as though you never existed, all in order to do the same to another person, family, organisation or entire society.

The aim of this book is to teach you how to guard the precious treasure of your own soul.

a tiny flame can illuminate the darkest room, and the deepest abyss can never overcome the light of a single candle.

KNOW THYSELF—KNOW THY PREDATOR

I magine you are a politician, or perhaps a housewife. An unemployed waiter, or the head of a major corporation. A television producer. A superficially self-righteous journalist. Maybe even a golf club committee member, a trade union activist, or perhaps the fun guy at the office who gets on with everyone and always has a cheeky smirk on his face.

Now imagine that one morning you wake up to discover that you have lost any sense of empathy towards all other human beings, animals, and the world in general. More than this, you also find upon waking that your ability for compassion and love has also departed, along with any understanding of another human being's emotional depth. Suddenly, you find yourself in a world of your own, devoid of morals, ethics, remorse, and accountability as well as any meaningful affection for other living things.

Upon the realisation that you are no longer 'burdened' with the capacity to care about the welfare of others, you still retain the ability to observe examples of compassion and emotional richness amongst other humans and then *mimic those emotions*. It dawns on you: you have now *detached,* and unlike the rest of the world you are no longer at the mercy of *needing* to care about anyone else. You sense some tremendous 'power' in this, and it's intoxicating. This new, remorseless advantage coupled with the sense of power may just be the most thrilling experience you have ever known and — like any addict — you find yourself greedy for more.

Guilt is no longer your problem. You are now freed from the

morality and empathy that shackles the rest of society. There is no pointer in your moral compass. You are a clandestine and feral entity within a domesticated landscape and you are the only one who knows this secret power you now carry inside.

You have witnessed other people displaying this thing called compassion and find it is now a concept completely foreign to your nature, along with emotional bonding, love and a deep-rooted affection for other living entities. You observe the effects of some apparent unspoken agreement amongst other humans concerning the sacredness of life, personal respect and human rights granted towards others — you get the general concept, sure — but you have no idea what it is to bond emotionally, nor feel empathy for another living thing. You simply do not fully understand what this must feel like. You are aware — at least in principle — what is it to mimic compassion for other human beings. *"Yeah!"* you think, *"I can fake that!"*

Then you get out of bed and you look into the mirror. What you see staring back at you is **a socialised psychopath**. You are now ready to prey on others.

However, you did not really wake up one morning like this — this is how you have been from the moment you left your mother's womb. All humanity has been your quarry ever since you ceased suckling at her loving breast and began eating solid food. Your performance has been centre-stage among the gullible and the oblivious that you fool endlessly with your never-ending parade of social masks and invented personas, all tailor-made to manipulate whomever, wherever and however it takes to serve your advantage.

When you finally get what you want from your chosen target, they have served their purpose. A new role for you beckons and you discard them like old stage makeup. The rush of energy you harvest from the emotional (and often financial) trail of misery, confusion and unanswered questions left in your wake recharges you and fills you with excitable giddiness. If there was an Oscar for Best Performance for Fake Multiple Personality you would win it every day of your life. Every tear your victims shed is akin to another bottle of celebratory champagne being uncorked. You love it. You adore your ability to manipulate others. In your estimation, if they are destroyed, it is their own fault — *they were weak.* Your sociopathic star shines in the faces of all you blind and you love to bathe in the dazzling light of its narcissistic glow.

You are the producer, the writer, the choreographer, the set designer and leading star in a Broadway sensation of your own making which always plays to a full house and closes whenever you decide. You are a psychopath, and tender prey is everywhere, eagerly awaiting you to stalk and devour them.

But your final curtain call and your star on the Walk of Infamy is always much closer than you bargained for…

This book represents the result of many year's study into human pathology brought about by several first-hand encounters with psychopaths — via the workplace and being involved in political organisations, through to the wider social and corporate levels and along with my own personal involvement with psychopaths and sociopaths (the two most commonly used terms for the same personality type) within a personal relationship. I have long been fascinated with psychopaths, though I have to admit for most of my life I had no idea what they truly were. Images of serial killers or cult leaders were the first thing to pop into my mind, but now when I use the terms *psychopath, psychopathic* and *psychopathology* I refer to the everyday, socially-adept psychopathic individuals who live amongst us, for these make up the overwhelming majority of psychopaths in the world today.

I choose the term *psychopath* for two reasons: *sociopath* or *narcissist* are commonly used to describe the same pathology, but since *psychopath* is the term usually applied by the leading professionals researching this subject it feels right to do so as well for the purposes of this book. An even more compelling reason is that most psychopaths — due to their warped egocentric grandiosity — prefer to be called either *sociopaths* or *narcissists* because they think these terms may make them seem less insane. Appearances are everything to a psychopath.

Since I consider these individuals to be the most deranged predators on the planet, I'm not interested in watering down their pathology by using a term more acceptable to *them* to serve their misguided hope that being called 'a narcissist' may some day lead to public acceptance of their behaviour. Calling a psychopath 'a narcissist' is akin to calling a rapist 'a selfish lover'.

In December 2010 it was announced that the new version of the Diagnostic Statistical Manual (DSM) — the handbook for mental health professionals — will no longer contain Narcissistic Personality Disorder (NPD). This is a very positive development which helps clear the waters in terms of clarity of thought when examining the subject with the aim of determining a valid and ethical diagnosis.

There is no part-time psychopath. They either are or are they are not. They are pure, undiluted and absolute. Anyone who has one or more pass through their lives knows this beyond a shadow of a doubt. We know for an absolute certainty that the demons have knocked at our door and a cold, toxic wind has passed over our souls that felt like nothing else we have experienced. It is the pure evil of the psychopath and if it were an element it would be plutonium. The devil really is in the details and one is never the same person after an encounter. Sometimes a creep is just a creep. However, only a psychopath is ever a psychopath.

The term *psychopath* carries with it a very powerful emotional resonance which really drives home the absolute toxic and malicious insidiousness of their machinations. Even on websites frequented by self-proclaimed psychopaths, they prefer not to use this term. The purpose of this book is not to indulge psychopaths and their grandiosity. If you have encountered, then discovered, and are now presently recovering from a psychopath, then the prospect of once more indulging what they may desire is probably the last thing on your to-do list anyway.

In the course of my own self-education I have discovered there is a tremendous number of people hungering for this information, along with a desire to gain practical knowledge concerning psychopaths, how they operate and how to recover from the devastation they leave in their wake. This is because we have all met them, even if we didn't at first realise what they were. They are the lowlifes, the serial womanisers, the shysters, the users, the abusers, the compulsive liars, the phonies and the fakes, and the damage they do can leave scars for a lifetime.

Billions of us on this planet also spend our daily lives directly under their control — either via psychopathic big business or at the hands of the many megalomaniac politicians. However, psychopaths most commonly rampage through our lives on a personal level, as incomprehensible and manipulative 'friends,' family members or spouses, or that vicious, relentless bully at work. They also appear in the guise of swindlers and con artists. All are devoid of any moral or ethical accountability for their actions and the damage they cause to others. This is the psychopath, and the only aspect of their nature which is pure and completely reliable is their negative and relentless predatory consciousness.

he who loves the least
controls the most.

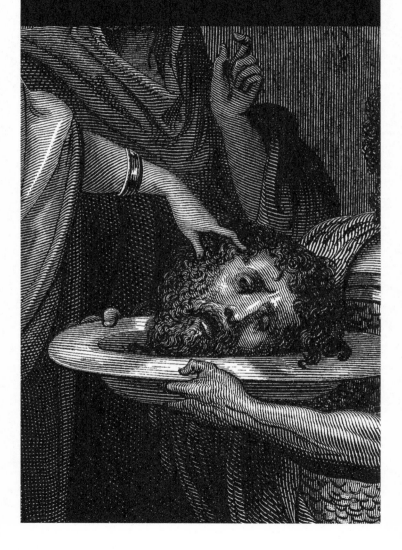

CHAPTER ONE
HOW DID WE GET HERE?

In spring 2008 I began working on a fictional horror novel set around the concept of demonically-possessed psychopaths working together as a hunting pack within a Wall Street investment bank. Putting the ideas for character development and storyline on various Internet message boards, I was astounded at how many otherwise straight-laced and ordinary people were willing to relate how their own encounters with psychopaths left them convinced that the psychopaths who victimised them were indeed demonically-possessed beings. Many of these people were not even religious and still they came to this conclusion, based solely upon their personal experience.

I was intrigued by what could make rational (and often very conservative) people living in the 21st century arrive at the belief that some individuals could have actual demons living inside them. In order to reach clarity, I began to devour every book, website and article I could on psychopaths and it began to dawn on me how common psychopaths actually are. What surprised me most of all was that despite the footprint of devastation they leave behind, I had managed to live with and work around them all my life without ever realising they'd been psychopaths from the start.

The term psychopath has been in common use since the 19th century and was popularised by psychiatrist Hervey Cleckley in his 1941 best seller *The Mask of Sanity: An Attempt to Clarify Some Issues About the So-Called Psychopathic Personality.* These self-serving, cold-blooded and psychologically vicious individuals I have en-

countered since childhood had all the behavioural and physiologi-
cal traits listed within the mainstream scientific diagnostic criteria
for evaluating psychopathic behaviour, yet I never considered any
of them to be a psychopath — and neither did most people who
knew them.

Why was this? For starters, they did not look like Jason from the
Friday the 13th movies, yet there was no doubt that all these lowlifes, charmers, bullies and con artists — including people I knew
personally who walked out on their spouses and children like they
never existed — were indeed psychopaths.

They had all the traits consistent with the pathology, excluding
a chainsaw and an ice hockey mask; and suddenly the world was
a different place for me. The commonly-held notion that all people have some good in them went out the window. I then began to
take a closer look at many leaders in politics and corporations and
at various other public figures and the inevitable penny began to
drop...

My research into uncovering the underlying root causes of psychopathy ended in frustration. Much of the research that goes
into determining what makes a psychopath become a psychopath
seemed vague, contradictory and even skewed with politically-
correct agendas. The genetic aspects also seemed inconclusive and
speculative. Psychopathic children are born to non-psychopathic
parents, and psychopathic parents often have non-psychopathic
children. It is as if the psychopathic consciousness simply seems
to arrive in a human body for no specific reason at the time of their
birth, in most cases.

Sometimes, psychopathic parents can indeed encourage pathological behaviour in their non-psychopathic children, psychologically and emotionally sculpting them as a type of proto-psychopath. We see this throughout history with the psychopathic elite
and so-called aristocratic bloodlines.

Many of the early studies into the pathology were incredibly
class-ridden and often racist, bandying about terms such as 'moral insanity' and 'moral imbecility' aimed at poor and immigrant

groups while ignoring the far more destructive and far-reaching psychopathic mindset of the wealthy ruling classes. This, I believe, was by design, and it still goes on today. The desire to fence off psychopathic behaviour amongst the poor and disadvantaged went very much in line with the Darwinian concept of 'survival of the fittest' which the social elite embraced and promoted in order to 'scientifically' underpin their self-professed right to rule over the rest of us.

What academics of yesteryear referred to as 'moral insanity' and 'moral imbecility' among the poor can be easily exchanged for the terms 'colonial expansion' and 'manifest density' spouted by the same elite families who still control the purse strings of nearly all modern-day scientific and medical research. For close to one hundred years now, the elite have attempted to cultivate a social consensus that the more socially marginalised an individual is, the more likely they are to be psychopathic simply due to their 'poor pedigree'. Nothing could be further from the truth.

From the Medici family of Florence from the 12th century up to the late Renaissance, and in many other powerful clans both historical and contemporary, psychopathic behaviour is fostered within the children in order for the dynastic power base of the family to continue to hold and maintain influence over others. Lack of empathy and brutal domination over 'inferiors' is encouraged within their 'privileged' offspring. Humans who may otherwise have grown up to be normal, empathic people. However, they are still not psychopaths. These people may eventually feel deep regret for what they did to others. On the other hand, a true psychopath, regardless of social status, race or gender has absolutely no conscience, remorse, guilt or empathy, *ever*.

What makes a psychopath a psychopath? We may never fully resolve the answer to this question, and certainly not with a purely scientific approach. But psychopaths are here and we have to deal with them, along with the often horrific emotional and psychological impact they have on our lives. Once resolved, it is then our responsibility to move on from the experience to become wiser and more complete individuals.

YE SHALL KNOW THE TREE BY ITS FRUIT

The universally accepted underlying characteristic of psychopathic behaviour is muted emotional responses to negative situations in combination with often unrestrained impulsiveness. In clinical evaluations, this basic psychopathic archetype can be determined with neuroimaging technology and/or psychological evaluation and testing. As we will see, however, clusters of psychopathic behaviours and traits along with social and personal interaction are the main determining factors in identifying psychopathology in others. Fortunately, when one becomes skilled in recognising these traits and pathologies, psychopath-spotting becomes relatively straightforward. Developing this ability will serve you as a highly useful skill in maintaining a less stressful and less angst-ridden life.

As they pass puberty, psychopaths become aware that they are not 'normal' in terms of their emotional depth and range of feelings. They then make a conscious or unconscious decision to capitalise on this emotional vacuum within them, and use it to exploit and manipulate others. They see this not only as a means of social survival, but in many cases also as a free ticket to piggyback and leap-frog on the efforts and talents of others. They are the ultimate human parasite. Psychopaths have no shame or guilt, nor indeed do they consider themselves burdened by their pathology; rather they view it as a tremendous gift.

The predatory nature of the psychopath never changes and remains with the psychopath until they die. There is no cure for a psychopath and if asked, the overwhelming majority of psychopaths would tell you they are perfectly fine with their pathology. They view it as a fantastic advantage. They consider themselves feral and free.

They do make a point of not informing the rest of us of their emotional emptiness and predatory intent, and herein lies the problem: when an empathic person meets the psychopath there is no level playing field. The psychopath has all the clandestine advantage required to exploit the victim's human decency and empathy.

THE LUNATICS ARE (MOSTLY) RUNNING THE ASYLUM

We live in a world essentially aligned with psychopathology, yet few people are aware of this reality and instead consider it 'normal,' or 'just the way things are'. Skewed by Hollywood and popular media, the common image of how a psychopath operates in day-to-day life is a long way off the mark. In this book, I hope to undo the colossal ignorance of what psychopaths really are, while also highlighting the often unpunished damage they inflict upon individuals and society as a whole. Psychopaths may not be demonically possessed *as such*, but beyond question, they are not motivated by a human consciousness.

Not coming from an academic background allows me certain liberties that are not available to mental health professionals or other accredited experts, who would have to hold back from public statements regarding the all-encompassing **Psychopathic Control Grid** under which we are currently forced to live. I am not dependent upon government or corporate research grants and therefore can refrain from self-censorship when highlighting the obvious psychopathic behaviour of certain public figures and institutions. By contrast, in many of the books and academic journals written by accredited professionals on psychopaths, one gets the sense that they are biting their collective tongues in order to restrain what they really want to say and what conclusions they have really drawn about psychopathology as a whole. Understandably, they have careers and professional reputations to consider since — very often — it is the powerful psychopaths *who issue their pay cheques*.

I don't have this dilemma : I will use my non-academic licence to draw the conclusions which I believe should be put out there for consideration.

Psychopaths are far too dangerous to be ignored or stereotyped into triviality and fiction. Allowing certain aspects of psychopathic influence and destruction to be overlooked or filed away under 'not for discussion' in the sense of what may or may not fit with lab-endorsed empirical evidence is simply something I cannot walk away from.

To any who may question the validity of my research and findings, my answer would be that a victim of child abuse does not need to obtain a PhD in Human Biology in order to understand the impact of paedophiles or have the ability to recognise them later on in life. I am writing this book as a survivor who has backed up his assertions with meticulous research. Make of it what you will; I am just a messenger. Use your own discernment regarding the validity of the message and how it might resonate with your own experience.

Some of the information within this book was given to me directly from self-confessed psychopaths themselves during conversations and email exchanges. I have also compiled recollections of working directly with psychopaths, including a 'friendship' with an investment banker who was a self-admitted psychopath and told me so in as many words. Other information and testimonies were given to me by victims who shared uncannily identical experiences with psychopaths regardless of their age, gender, geographic location or relationship to the psychopath. The bulk of this book, however, is based largely on my own close observation from my time working in Wall Street investment banks and the music industry, along with the studies and findings of mental health professionals and others which I found relevant and worthy of sharing within these pages.

This book is not a crusade against the psychopaths who exist and prey among all strata of society. Nor am I promoting violence against psychopaths, except in the case of immediate self-defence. I am not even advocating 'getting even with them' outside the domain of the courts. You'll never get even, and the psychopath does not care. You will die looking for revenge and all the while the psychopath who damaged you *will not care one iota*. You stand in danger of becoming engulfed in a toxic quagmire of pointless retribution, grasping for straws of revenge, while the psychopath will have simply moved on to his or her next target(s) as though you — the previous 'useful idiot' — never existed. The psychopath does not care. They will never admit they were wrong and mean it. They will never tell you that you are right and mean it. They will never be the person you thought you fell in love with or shared personal or professional plans with. They will never take responsibility for your well-being or comfort or peace of mind. They *do not care, do not care, do not care* — so now *you have to stop caring about the psychopath.*

The purpose of this book is to help readers become aware of psychopaths and their traits and then — if victimised — garnish a positive outlook from the experience. That's it. Recognise and then get away, then regain and restore yourself while using your new-found wisdom and maturity to become a better you. Psychopaths cannot be cured, reformed, understood or rehabilitated and more important, *they see no reason why they should be.* As incredible as it may sound to normal people, this is the cold, harsh reality of the pathology.

Sometimes, the only way to win is not to play.

MARRIED WITH CHILDREN

One of the most difficult situations is when you are trapped in a psychopathic marriage with children involved, and you are concerned about leaving your children with the psychopath. Counselling is impossible since the psychopathic spouse is a compulsive liar who will use these sessions to learn how to manipulate you more effectively. As this is a very complicated issue and everyone's personal circumstances are different, my only suggestion would be to begin developing a legal exit strategy to leave the relationship while safeguarding the financial and psychological well-being of your children. Finding a support network of friends and sympathetic relatives who will let you live in their homes for an extended period without judging you is a must. Hiding money away in a secret account (cash is best) until you have enough to finance your getaway is also vital.

Endlessly make secret provisions for your escape and if the only option is to leave your children for a while, then up until the very moment of departure *continually express your love and devotion to them*, then on the eve of your departure tell them how much you love them and how you will be with them again soon when the problems are sorted out. Do not try to character-assassinate the psychopath spouse when talking to the children. The psychopath will be doing this constantly to them about you and the last thing you want is to make your children become the rope in a tug-of-war.

However, the truth about the psychopathic spouse will come out eventually, so you may in all likelihood have to live with consequences of the psychopath implementing a vicious and heartless smear campaign against you to your own children. It will hurt deeply, but you will have the final word eventually. Do not use the children as pawns — they will be dealing with this tactic from your ex-spouse and it is the last thing they need. Think everything over carefully, do what you can for the children and then leave, trusting that it will all work out in the end.

Taking Care of Business

Contrary to popular assumptions, psychopaths very rarely have a physically sadistic or vindictive malice against you personally. With a psychopath, *it is just business*. You had something they wanted and they came after it. It may have been anything from your money to your sexual organs, or your vote or taking your position at work away from you, or marrying you/getting pregnant for no other reason than they needed a place to live after they were thrown out of their last accommodation. *Just business* — along with the rush of power they enjoyed while they had you fooled and psychologically disorientated.

Avoidance of psychopaths is the message here, but if the demon has already knocked on your door and you have invited them in, deal with the experience as best you can and then move on. Chances are you'll get a lot from the encounter in the long term, but only if you fully understand what you are dealing with.

One must also bear in mind that people often willingly enter into long-term relationships with psychopaths, because they turned a blind eye to certain 'red flags' present during the relationship/involvement. This is not to downplay the trauma of innocent victims who may have been slowly lured into the labyrinth of the psychopath over a period of years. This experience is common and is essentially the hallmark of the psychopath with the patience to mind-control their victim in precise, incremental stages through a see-saw effect of cruel/loving performances. However, even in these cases the victims often know deep down inside that they should leave, but make complex excuses to themselves as to why they should not.

The question has to be asked: what prevents the victim from ending the relationship? There is a profound moment of realisation that all victims of psychopaths have to reach in order to fully recover from the experience. It wasn't the victim's fault they became ensnared to begin with, though many will admit they remained with the psychopath longer than they should have.

I come from the viewpoint that either consciously or subconsciously, we invite these psychopaths into our lives. There is a reason for this, and a lesson for all of us to learn. We need to evolve both psychologically and emotionally — as individuals and as a society. We have no choice. It is time to grow up. We must begin to see psychopaths as pawns who are here to *serve us* and not become permanently lost in our own endless cycle of victim complexes and self-pity.

The reason I believe that psychopaths appear to be so prevalent in Western society today is that we, collectively, have it too easy, and in the modern world there is a growing and profoundly unnatural infantilism among many adults. As a consequence of this 'maturity vacuum', personal and social evolutionary necessity will bring the psychopath into our lives in order to 'shake up' our often comfortable, molly-coddled complacency.

Our materialistic and social development has long overtaken our psychological and spiritual maturity. This **Psychopathic Control Grid** has been very much by design via social engineering and mass psychological conditioning through media, politics and public education. We need to regain our emotional, psychological and spiritual independence. We have to learn that we do not need to keep externalising ourselves as a matter of social obligation in order to feel 'complete'. As Terence McKenna said, *"Culture is not your friend."*

My personal belief after dealing with psychopaths is that they serve an important function in society. From the manipulative and highly-successful politician to the remorseless CEO, to the neighbour who attempts to weasel the elderly and vulnerable out of their money and homes — the bottom line is we might actually *need* psychopaths.

This may seem a shocking statement to many people, especially to any readers of this book who are in the early stages of recovery from a psychopathic encounter, but upon reflection we have to understand that psychopaths may enter our lives to light a much-needed fire under our personal and collective backsides.

After a psychopath has ravaged through our life we must process the experience. Once identified, we must — as a matter of extreme urgency and for the sake of our psychological well-being and personal safety — *ignore and shun the psychopath* **FOREVER**, and then move on. What happens to the psychopath is no longer our concern. The two ships have passed in the night, and we should take a page from the psychopath's own rule-book and *turn our entire focus within ourselves*; only in our case, we do it to address any possible shortcomings within our own personalities that may have attracted the experience in the first place.

If we do not learn this lesson then we are doomed to repeat it.

Psychopaths cannot help being psychopaths, but they can control their behaviour. The neurological/electrical systems in their brains, as a part of their pathology, is so completely distorted that they have no other recourse than to make whatever life they can for themselves. However, they do know 'right' from 'wrong' and this knowledge makes them powerful. The ability to casually undertake the most appalling acts, to be aware of the intensity of the situation and not give a damn, is why they are not 'unwell people who need our love and support'.

Psychopaths are very aware of what they are doing and why, and even when driven by impulse they will not flinch from doing the same thing over and over again with a succession of victims. They are thrilled by the excitement and rush they get from destroying human hearts and lives. The psychopath is not an unwell person who deserves pity, *this is a monster*, a demon from whom you run away as soon as you recognise it for what it is — *even if the monster is your own flesh and blood*.

Psychopaths can be very successful if they have real intellect and charm, not to mention that 'glow' which many of them have due to their high testosterone levels. Other psychopaths remain bottom feeders who have neither the talent nor intellect to get beyond swindling the oblivious. We have all encountered them. From romantic liaisons, to the workplace, to ticking a box next to the psychopath's name on polling day. Ignorance of the psychopath has been a huge disadvantage for most of us — making us easy prey. Psychopaths are one of the few genuine examples of when we can exclaim, *"I didn't see it coming!"* and it rings completely true.

Psychopaths cause colossal social, psychological and financial problems throughout society and do this without any guilt or feelings of remorse. So, what's the point in trying to 'get even'? Better to come to terms with their condition and just avoid them. They don't care about you, and once you get over a psychopath, why should you care about them? If there are legal issues involved then let the courts deal with it.

Get on with your life and take from the experience what you can.

Deprogramming Oneself

Before we delve further into the labyrinth, we must first cast off several popular misconceptions that many of us have about the world and the human race in general. These include:

That all people have some good in them.

That all people are capable of love and of being loved.

That all people instinctively know right from wrong, good from bad, justice from injustice, and follow these behaviours for the same reasons most of us do during the course of our lives.

That psychopaths are always and only bug-eyed, twitching axe murderers who enjoy hands-on killing.

That all psychopaths are — at first sight any-way — creepy-looking-and-behaving individuals.

That *you* are not mind-controlled by mass media, politics and social requirements, and that most of your thoughts, assumptions and personal and political beliefs are your own.

Got that? Now let's begin looking for the way out of this maze and understand how we ended up here in the first place.

WHY DOES IT HURT SO DIFFERENTLY THIS TIME?

One aspect of the post-psychopath experience is how victims actually mourn the end of a relationship as if it were *a death*. There is a reason for this: a death *has* occurred. The fake persona manufactured to 'work you' has been killed off by the same psychopath who invented it.

People who emerge from a psychopathic relationship also ask themselves why the effects are so traumatic and seem to border on emotional rape. Everyone has been dumped, though people get over this in time. However with a psychopath it is often hard to express how 'different' it feels.

In the early days of the relationship, the psychopath plays on the victim's nurturing/parental needs with the 'little boy lost' or 'hurt little girl' performance, stirring up deep-rooted feelings of parental obligation within the victim. When this is applied to adults who may have no children of their own, the consequences for the victims are horrifically emotionally convulsive after the psychopath decides to no longer 'play the game'.

Companion personas are also utilised for financial gain by predator psychopaths who target elderly people living alone. Agencies who provide carers for elderly clients often have to go to extreme lengths in order to weed out psychopaths who use the profession to find targets. This is a huge problem for these agencies.

In terms of the psychopathic home care worker, they will seek out elderly persons *with no family*. The psychopath will always initially cultivate trust with the elderly person and become a kind of surrogate family member. The psychopath will then move in and begin living rent-free with the eventual aim to become the inheritor of the victim's estate. Alcohol and medication can be slipped into drinks in order to keep the elderly person oblivious to their predicament. This drugging of the victim is used to emulate or worsen dementia, with the aim of moving the elderly person into a nursing home rather than causing death. This gives the psychopath full stewardship of the elderly victim's home. Occasionally, this pernicious agenda is discovered by neighbours or other care workers/doctors who notice that the elderly person becomes neglected/reclusive even though the carer has moved into the house full time to 'look after them' around the clock.

The concerned neighbours will often then alert the local authorities. This results in the psychopath having a sudden change of lifestyle and relocating to another region with little prior warning. Generally, a new relationship they have found on the Internet provides the escape route for the psychopath. Meanwhile, the victim will be left wondering where their surrogate child has gone, and usually misses them very deeply. Even if the fraud is uncovered and prevented, the trauma inflicted on the elderly person is profoundly damaging and painfully humiliating.

Thus, when a relationship (often including a romantic attachment) ends with the psychopath, it has the same emotional impact on victims as losing a loved one through death. The psychopath manipulates the victim's subconscious parental/romantic desires to become a kind of surrogate child or lover, and then they symbolically 'die'. That's why a break-up with a psychopath feels so different. It was *planned by them to be this way all along*. It happens very quickly, taking the victim completely by surprise.

Psychopaths always use pity as a tool to ensnare caring, nurturing and/or lonely people as enablers. Destroying their fake persona results in the psychopath becoming essentially an animated corpse in the eyes of the victim, further compounding the horror of the experience. It stirs something very primal in their victims, who feel like, *'This person should be dead, yet they are smug, jovial and alive! What is wrong with this picture!?'* The psychopath has murdered the fake persona they invented, yet it is very much a real death to the person the psychopath has manipulated. But in the case of this sort of 'death,' there is no funeral, no grieving ritual, no grave and often no one able to adequately comfort and support the victim.

In many ways, the abandonment of the persona is almost like a form of self-sacrifice for the psychopath — a symbolic death of sorts, but a sacrifice offering the 'reward' of being reborn as a phoenix rising from the ashes. One has to wonder if there is more to this than just working a new scam or if the psychopath is also attracted to the *tabula rasa* of leaving everything behind, and if there is some exhilaration in the process that becomes addictive? Personally, I believe they harvest some kind of emotional energy from their victims. I came to this conclusion having witnessed psychopaths literally light up with a strange effervescent excitability in the aftermath of a 'win,' as though they had been plugged into some kind of unconscious power source and were instantly recharged by it.

It has to take some effort to keep one or more fake personas functional for any length of time — even the most spectacularly successful psychopath must find some exertion in the experience. Likewise, there also has to be a tremendous sense of relief in their persona self-annihilation. Many people remark that not only do psychopaths express neither shame nor guilt when they move on, but they also seem to have the aspect of having a weight lifted off their shoulders; this is perhaps why a psychopath can seem giddy and chipper between personas. They have bought themselves some time to recharge their batteries before beginning a new role. The psychopath may experience the destruction of their previous persona as a form of climax to the performance. Following this, they have the fresh excitement of researching new ways to manipulate the next victim. The cycle continues.

Is it any wonder that the ending of a relationship with a psychopath is so intensely traumatic for victims? The best way for victims to deal with this experience is to imagine the psychopath as a dead person in the grave. The *No Contact Ever Again* rule is vital towards accomplishing this.

FOUR LITTLE LETTERS: N, C, E & A

There is only one rule to follow upon realising someone you know is a psychopath:

NO CONTACT EVER AGAIN.

There is no grey area in this approach. Once you have identified the predator, you must walk away from them and leave them for good. Do not be concerned about hurting their feelings — a psychopath does not have access to the same emotions you do and consequently they cannot be really 'hurt.' You were never anything other than an object to them. You may have provided them with everything from social status to putting a roof over their head, but you were never a human being to them. All their 'love' was fake — a performance to manipulate you.

If the psychopath walks away from you, then the NCEA rule still applies. The person you thought the psychopath was is *a persona only* and remains nothing other than a carefully-crafted piece of theatre designed to 'work you'. That persona is now obsolete to the psychopath, and any promise the persona made that you still hope may be fulfilled has long since been discarded by the psychopath as irrelevant.

If you are mourning 'the good old days,' remember that what

you think you miss is not the person but *the persona*. The psychopath who created the persona is a murderer — of your hopes, your dreams, your faith, belief and trust, and above all, of the manipulative persona they created just for you.

The NCEA rule also includes blocking psychopaths from your Twitter/Facebook accounts, instant messaging, phone numbers and all other personal access to you, in the same way you act decisively to keep your kitchen free from cockroaches or your attic free from rats. It has nothing to do with being vindictive or spiteful. You are dealing with a pest that endangers your health and quality of life.

After you implement the NCEA rule, you may find yourself having vivid and highly symbolic dreams about the psychopath. One woman who contacted me through my YouTube channel told me she had dreams about the psychopath which were unlike any dreams she ever had in her life—very intense and loaded with metaphor. Others have told me that the psychopaths themselves never actually appear in the dreams, but scenarios where the psychopath is expected to arrive yet never does, are common. This is your subconscious mind telling you that the longed-for person never existed to begin with. Keeping a dream diary or journal during this period can aid greatly with the healing process.

Understand that the initial aftershocks of a relationship with a psychopath is almost identical to the symptoms suffered by people with Post Traumatic Stress Disorder, especially if you were in a long-term relationship with the psychopath. This can be particularly painful for parents of psychopathic adult children. Flesh and blood means nothing to the psychopath other than being a potentially useful back-up plan should the need arise. A psychopathic adult child is not capable of being loved or giving love and they will not be emotionally damaged by you disowning them. They don't care other than they may have to find someone else to constantly bail them out. This often results in the psychopath finding an enabler to marry soon afterwards.

It is also important to sever any material links you may have back to the psychopath. Psychopaths hate the NCEA strategy because it puts them in the position of no longer having any control over their victims, and no pernicious pathway back into their lives. Often, the psychopath will leave items of value with the victim; perhaps books, antiques, or keepsakes that belonged to a deceased parent. You must mail these items back to the psychopath ASAP. If you cannot locate the psychopath's new whereabouts, sell the items and give the money to charity. If it comes down to dumping them in the trash, then do it.

The psychopath's mother's photo album has no real sentimental value to the psychopath at all — they leave belongings in your home as method of re-establishing contact should the need arise, and they will use it as an excuse to re-enter your life as though they are waving a promissory note. Once the psychopath abandons you, *you are not responsible for their possessions or any gifts they presented you with*. Neither should you consider these objects as keepsakes — looking at them will bring up memories and feelings which are toxic and will pollute your soul. This is partly the reason the psychopath left them with you.

The psychopath might bury a dead pet of theirs in your garden (making a big performance of the event) so they always have a reason to come and visit later and you'll be placed in the awkward position of having to defend your humanity by *not letting them come to your house*. Know this: the dead dog or cat was buried in your garden for this very reason. You owe the psychopath nothing. They are not coming to grieve their beloved pet, they are testing and tugging the 'hook' they have in you.

If they painted the walls of your house blue, then repaint them white. Destroy all physical traces of their existence — all they will do is drain your emotional energy and remind you of the vampiric nature of the psychopath. The psychopath committed persona-suicide when they decided to no longer play a certain role to manipulate you, and what use does a 'dead person' have for their stuff? They chose to kill off their persona — let them deal with ALL the consequences of doing this. They want to play dead, then fair enough — let's play the game completely.

Once you have implemented the *No Contact Ever Again* rule you are on the path to recovery. Learn from the experience and you will have a fuller and more meaningful life in the long run. The only good psychopath is one which is nowhere near you.

LOUISE'S STORY

"From the moment I met Kyle, my soon-to-be ex-husband—whom I now believe to be a classic sociopath/psychopath, he seemed gentle, loving and caring and was liked by everyone. When we first met, he had just returned home from his military service with the US Marines after seventeen years away. During all those years, he never visited his family once. These years were mysterious and unknown to all who knew him. According to Kyle, he was in an elite group 'Recon Marines' and was on-call around the clock. During the short vacations he took, a few days here and there, he visited other cities and countries.

All those seventeen years he was stationed in Okinawa, Japan. He said that they allowed him to stay in Japan because he was fluent in Japanese. He claimed to have served as translator between the US Marines and the Japanese government. In fact, he is fluent in the Japanese language—however, seventeen years away from his family? A big red flag that troubled me, but like so many victims I willingly ignored it.

But the questions remained in my head … how come he didn't complete his twenty years service in order to collect his full retirement pay? He claimed he was discharged after a confrontation with an officer. Had lost his career and everything attached to it—benefits and all. When we met he was living with his parents and he didn't even have a car. He told me that he was putting his life together and he wanted so much to prove this to me—and, he did!

So many things happened during the first year and ten months—he was consistently good. He became an apprentice plumber, went to trade school specializing in hi-tech heating systems. He was so dedicated to me and also dedicated to succeeding in his new career. He was always loving, caring and sweet. He made me the happiest I thought I could ever be. And on top of that, he was a good son, brother, and uncle too.

His father was diagnosed with cancer shortly after his return and Kyle held the family together. He was the one who took his father to each doctor visit, runs to the emergency rooms, and when his dad passed away he took care of all the funeral arrangements. Kyle was the rock of the family and a great comfort to his mother.

During that same time, other red flags surfaced that I again ignored. He told me that during his time in Japan he had become a Yakuza (Japanese Mafia) and that the son of the boss was his brother in the Yakuza as well as his closest friend. He also told me that he was in a Japanese prison for one year for drug trafficking and he also told me that all that was part of his past and with his departure from Japan they have let him go with no attachments. Yes, huge red flags, but I was so much in love at that point.

He told me that this was the third phase of his life. First phase; Kyle was raised in a low income neighbourhood with a lot of issues and criminality where he was involved in gangs. Second phase; Kyle joined the military to make something of himself and leave the bad environment of his growing years. Third phase; Kyle's returning home to the USA and finding me so we could build a new life together. I thought to myself. "The past is past and everyone deserves a second chance," And why not, he was doing so incredibly well!

Things started deteriorating after the death of Kyle's father. We were three months away from our wedding date and living together. He became very obsessed with me and acting like he was in a war zone—yes, 'crazy-making' indeed. He would put traps around the house, and hide tape recorders claiming that I was cheating on him. He would stand on guard all night with a gun and even claimed to inject himself with steroids in order to stay awake.

I was very scared and cried every day not knowing what to do. I thought about breaking off the engagement, but I had already a promise of love and if he was grieving the death of his father—was this a sort of Post Traumatic Stress Disorder (PTSD) taking him to the emotional pain of memories of the war zone? I needed to be there for him. I even kept quiet from everyone that one night he actually pointed a loaded revolver at me.

Slowly, things started to improve again and we made it through the wedding. During our honeymoon, Kyle recognized that something was wrong with him and would ask every night if I could see the shadows on the ceiling. I would tell him there are no shadows, and that he was going to be okay. And, yes, he indeed "recuperated" with time and with my loving compassion and support.

We moved into our new home that we bought with the proceeds from the sale of my condominium—he was driving a new car, which we bought with the sale of my old car. Didn't bother me at that time—he was working hard and doing great in his new career.

Between 2005 and the beginning of 2008, life was good. We loved our home. Kyle became a fully-licensed plumber, and he was still performing as the good man. I remember telling him, every day. "I love you honey, you are the best husband and the best man in the world," to which he often responded, "No, I am not. I sold my soul to the devil a long time ago." Yes, that troubled me, but I always thought that it was the pain of his time in war conflicts. I was trying to be so understanding.

In the Spring of 2008, the full horror started to unfold. He started growing impatient and could be so rude—snapping at me in ways he never did before and for minor things. He started working long hours and wouldn't get home until 10PM. According to him, he was doing small jobs on the side in addition to his regular job. Kyle went away four weekends in a row to work in Martha's Vineyard—an island off the coast of Massachusetts. Claiming that the island didn't have plumbers that could service the hi-tech boilers. However, things didn't feel right. Beginning in

2008, from time to time, I just couldn't connect with him. There was something dark, mysterious, and ugly that kept me away, but I didn't know what.

In August of 2008 the nightmare exploded into full scale horror. It was a beautiful Sunday morning and we were just waking up. I told him "I love you honey, you are the best husband in the world." He looked away and said, "No, I am not. I kissed another woman. I'm sorry I had to..." I responded, "What? When? Why did you have to?"

Well, supposedly he had received calls from the Yakuza family and he was active again. I felt that my life had fallen apart in just one second in that moment. He told me that he needed to leave the house for a couple of weeks to do what he needed to do and that he would talk to the boss to ask him for a release. He said that he was never let go, but put on a period of "rest".

Two weeks went by, but then he needed another two weeks, because he was given a list of eight people to eliminate. Kyle now claimed he was a hit man for the Yakuza. He needed to be away from home to keep me safe. I was completely horrified and scared. I would cry every day, and right up until the present my hands still can't stop shaking. He would remark that he 'didn't know how to look at me,' from the shame of what he was doing. In November, he stopped coming home though from time to time he would call or text me.

Between August of 2008 and October of 2009, I lived like a prisoner in my house alone, hiding from my friends, staying quiet to my family, crying in terror for my life in the basement of my home. I would only go out to go to work and then return home. I got antidepressants through my doctor, and no one could tell that something was happening in my life. In the meantime, Kyle told me that the Yakuza wanted him to prepare a guy to take his place before they could let him go and that he was living in safehouses and sometimes in his shop.

In June 2009, he stop helping me financially and I was carrying all the financial burden and responsibilities of the house. Receiving collectors' calls from credit cards providers I didn't even know he had, I paid most of them — including the credit card he used to buy the jewellery that with so much 'love' he gave to me as presents.

Why did I go along with this? I thought he was in danger. I believed that he was trapped. He claimed that with the downturn of the economy there were not many jobs and he was not receiving payroll payments. Plus he was not getting anything from the other job because he didn't want to owe anything to them and that he just wanted to be let go.

In October of 2009, I decided that I couldn't take it anymore and needed to find out what was really happening — things didn't add up. Trying to be the good wife and with my values of respect, I never touched any piece of mail he received except for bills. Well after a year, I opened each one of them and what did I find out? Charges to restaurants and female stores, and cancelled checks for the rent of an apartment on a building no more than a mile away from my home. Oh yes, I was mad. I took my copy of the car key, went there and searched the car. What did I find? A copy of his apartment lease dated November 2008, a female hat, the picture of a young woman in a bathtub and one female shoe.

I confronted him and according to Kyle the woman was a prostitute that he was using for his mafia activities, but that he didn't have anything to do with her. The female shoe was a mistake on the clean-up on the disposing of a body. And the apartment, he didn't live there, it was all to disguise and to keep me disconnected from him to keep me safe. And, the apartment was being paid by the mafia. OMG I was a mess! He was so convincing that I believed him at that moment. My life! What do I do? Went back to my basement and cried, but that did not stop me and I started my own little investigation. I needed to find the truth, but everything was confusing and I was scared for my life.

(1) Kyle's mother and sister actually attested to the fact that he was a made man for the Yakuza. His sister told me once, "Poor Louise, she didn't know that when she married my brother, she married the Godfather!" She was laughing

and I was in shock. That event happened while having dinner the day following the morning when Kyle told me that he had been called to do a hit — it was my birthday.

(2) He has two boys in Japan from a Japanese woman. The mother of the children is the 'half-sister' of his 'brother' in the 'Yakuza' family. The children think that Kyle is dead. The mother took them away from Kyle, supposedly, because she thought that Kyle was going to take them to the USA after his discharge — I have seen pictures of the boys.

(3) Kyle claims to be part of the 'Yamaguchi-gumi' family, considered the biggest and most dangerous Yakuza family.

(4) He does have a Yakuza type tattoo, which he got AFTER we were married. I also read a book on the Yakuza and I suspect Kyle's fabrications for being a hit man for them was based upon his reading the same book."

In Louise's testimony above we are provided with a classic initial insight into the everyday psychopath and their common methods of mind control and manipulation of their victims. This story is not as incredible as it first sounds — such experiences are very common for victims. First, the psychopath finds a compassionate and loving person to become their enabler who will suppress their intuition concerning the psychopath's mysterious past.

Using a combination of pity and pretend PTSD, the psychopath confuses and then emotionally/psychologically blurs the victim's increasing concerns. The psychopath then creates a false persona of a devoted and loving partner and goes to some lengths to prove this. Following this, an invented fake past to replace the previous mysterious past — an outrageous life story which cannot be easily verified and is often only backed up by family members who cannot verify the psychopath's story and are simply 'standing by their kin.'

Kyle's comments to Louise about his life being in stages is particularly insightful. The psychopath was literally outlining a blueprint, or script, for his own pathology. These stages were akin to roles played by an actor, which is exactly what was happening. Relationships with psychopaths always seem to come with their obligatory 'Life Phases' story, and victims are always made to believe they are a special element in all this. They make it sound so grand. However, psychopaths do not tell you their 'plans' are completely provisional, improvised and subject to change in an instant and without any prior warning.

The psychopath almost instantly commits adultery once married and — unlike a normal extra-marital fling — it takes place even when they are married to a loving and devoted person. How good-looking the spouse/victim is remains irrelevant to the psychopath. Many women who were discarded by psychopathic men are often shocked to find out the ex-boyfriend or husband left them for overweight/unattractive, much older/younger women or even left them *for another man.* The psychopath's reason for infidelity has nothing to do with falling for someone new or any serious marriage difficulties — it is a power game. The new relationship provides the psychopath with benefits or perks; only rarely are they purely sexual. Psychopaths are constantly having sex with just about anyone they can find and they are not particularly fussy about these chosen partners. It would be a responsible step to undergo a HIV or other STD test(s) when coming out of a relationship with someone whom you suspect may have been a psychopath.

The very common tactic seen in many male psychopaths is their need to present themselves as a James Bond-style individual — in Louise's case, a hit man for a Japanese mafia organisation. Made-up stories of being spies, secret agents, top secret military scientists who found out too much, or famous rock stars who had their legacy stolen are very common with male psychopaths.

To many people, Louise's story may seem far-fetched but the reality is millions of men and women around the world have been put through a similar experience, and often much, much worse. The psychopathic crazy-made world they inflict upon their victims is often so fantastically absurd that it becomes difficult for the victims to convey their personal stories to others; once the victim wakes up, they often stay silent for fear of being ridiculed and judged.

The ultimate message of Louise's story is that like many other victims of psychopaths, she suppressed her intuitions and ignored the red flags. This happened because her psychopathic husband seduced her into ignoring these signals.

Pay attention to your intuition and instincts — red flags are there for a reason. These natural skills have subconsciously spotted the psychopath for what they really are and exist to let you know that something just isn't right.

nothing is easier than to
denounce the evildoer;
nothing is more difficult
than to understand him.

Fyodor Dostoevsky

CHAPTER TWO
THE MARK OF THE BEAST

What makes a psychopath different from all other individuals? A psychopath goes through life leaving a trail of used-up victims, broken hearts, financial ruin, shattered hopes, destroyed organisations and entities, as well as a plethora of unfulfilled promises in their wake, and all this will be carried out by the psychopath without any consideration for consequences or moral responsibility. This is the fundamental difference unleashed upon individuals and society by the psychopath's true and essential nature.

A psychopath can be someone as basic as a slacker-type wastrel who looks for an easy life living off someone else's labours — usually an elderly relative, or a mind-controlled spouse or partner. They may not have an interest in taking anyone's money directly, *per se* — it is the power they feel from controlling the perceptions of others that remains the sum total of their parasitic ambitions.

Once they have a free roof over their heads, food in the refrigerator, heating in winter, and — more importantly — are not expected to do anything to contribute towards the mortgage and utility bills, then they are content with this arrangement. If the enabler becomes ill and cannot take care of the psychopath any longer, the psychopathic parasite simply finds another host to take over this role.

Psychopaths can also be ruthlessly ambitious despots who order the genocide of an entire ethnic group in order to double a nation's wool production in order to consolidate their power in office. The key thing all psychopaths have in common is power over the perceptions of others — whether it's a plumber with a part-time position in the Yakuza or a president who was elected on his high moral standing who also runs a sideline operation in human trafficking.

Many super-wealthy, aristocratic and powerful psychopaths love nothing better than to use their status and influence to 'repair' shortcomings they perceive in others. Usually, these same shortcomings and social problems *were created by the previous generation of like-minded influential and elite psychopaths*. Many of the elite of today are ordering the rest of us to reduce our carbon footprints while conducting interviews from their fuel-guzzling limos and private jets. They originate from the same aristocratic families who created the dependence upon oil in the first place. Naturally, they fail to see the irony in all this, and tellingly, they have used their bought-and-paid-for corporate media to blinker most of society from also recognising this irony.

The range of psychopathic traits in terms of the actual pathology itself can be anything and everything selfish, appalling, immoral and evil one can think of. A psychopath can manifest in any number of clustered pathologies and behavioural traits within a well-established framework of the psychopathic spectrum. I myself have lived with and among all sorts of small-time psychopaths, as well as worked with (in the music industry and Wall Street investment banks) all varieties of big-time psychopaths. I have also compiled notebooks full of information and observations taken from interviews with victims of psychopaths, as well as personal testimonies given to me by psychopaths themselves. Through this research I have come to recognise five key absolute traits which all psychopaths have in common. These are:

- No Remorse
- Invented Personas
- Invoking Pity in Others to Manipulate and Control
- Mysterious Pasts/Personal Histories
- High Levels of the Hormone Testosterone.

Along with these absolute traits, I have also identified a cluster of potential secondary or relative traits. Understanding and applying these criteria will go a long way to help one distinguish between psychopaths and everyday, run-of-the-mill obnoxious creeps and lowlifes. Once you come to understand and apply the absolute and relative trait lists, psychopath-spotting becomes straightforward.

I also cannot stress enough that one should not declare a person to be a psychopath unless you are completely sure you have fairly and honestly evaluated them with as much emotional neutrality as possible. **To use the label *psychopath* is essentially to state that they are not a human being. Such a statement — no matter how much someone may have wronged you — must not be taken lightly.**

Not every person who makes our lives miserable, acts like a creep, sleeps around on their partners/spouses, gets elected, runs a major corporation or engages in criminal activities is a psychopath. In the early days of recovery from an encounter it can become only too convenient to claim that anyone who has ever wronged you is or was a psychopath. We must bear in mind that over ninety-five percent of the human race are not psychopaths. A good number of these people have done terrible things in their lives, but they are still not psychopaths because they retain the desire for redemption.

The causes of criminal and anti-social behaviour are not always psychopathic, either. Nor are they even morally wrong in some cases. Many dictators and tyrants were overthrown by decent people who had no choice other than to become 'criminals' or 'terrorists'. Is a person who steals a loaf of bread to feed his children a psychopath? Of course not. Neither is a person who had an affair while their marriage was going through a rough patch. Life is complicated and we are subject to all the shortcomings and follies of the human condition. Some people are simply lazy slackers, or sexually promiscuous, or demonstrate poor or impulsive judgement and/or lack basic social skills, but these behaviours alone, without the other psychopathic traits, do not a psychopath make.

Being human, we contain *the potential for* the failings and follies of the human condition. This is normal, and as a result of our negative behaviour *we learn*, then decide to change for the better. The number one difference between the rest of us and a psychopath is *we feel bad about our past actions and any hurt we may have caused others*. We care that we wronged another person and ultimately attempt to find redemption and to make it up to them personally. We understand what empathy is and why being compassionate towards others is not only good for us as individuals, but serves all society as a whole. Compassion and empathy work; this is beyond doubt.

The difference is that psychopaths indulge in their negative and exploitative behaviour without a care in the world. Compassion and empathy are viewed by psychopaths as moronic traits. A psychopath sees empathy as a flaw and compassion as a weakness — flaws and weaknesses they then attempt to exploit for their own purposes.

The classic psychopath traits criteria was developed by Dr Robert Hare and is generally used as a standard guideline among mental health professionals and law-enforcement agencies when evaluating psychopathic behaviour. The *Hare Psychopathy Checklist, Revised* (PCL-R) outlines various psychopathic traits including glibness and superficial charm, cruelty to animals and an active refusal to take responsibility for one's actions. The main issue I have with the Dr Hare list (towards whom I have the utmost respect) is that it comes across as somewhat focussed towards the criminal/jailbird-type psychopath end of the spectrum. If you want to know the traits of the criminal psychopath who ends up in jail, then the PCL-R checklist is very good. However, its main stumbling block is that most psychopaths *are not in prison* and the majority of criminals in jail worldwide *are not psychopaths*.

Killing and torturing animals is also not as common as is often assumed among non-criminal psychopaths. Many in fact keep pets and utilise them for the practical benefits as well as using the pet to con others into seeing the psychopath as loving and trustworthy.

The psychopath can value the practical aspects of pets, such as guarding the house or catching mice, though they do not 'love' their pets any more than they love another human being. It's a hobby, manipulation tool, or useful social icebreaker for them. If they do kill an animal it is usually to eat it, or to avoid paying the veterinarian bills if they can not sucker someone else into paying for them.

Another aspect is that many psychopaths who are not impulsive petty thieves, killers and drug dealers locked up in prison are very capable of planning ahead and developing life goals which they have set for themselves. Dr Harold Shipman, the greatest psychopathic lone-wolf type serial killer in recorded history, did not become a qualified doctor on impulse. He had to complete an intensive medical education to earn his credentials before he could murder — by some estimates — more than four hundred people between 1974 and 1998.

It has to be said, though, that the vast majority of psychopaths do very poorly in formal education and genuine career advancement. Most are technically and cognitively extremely incompetent, though they project an image of a 'hotshot' or 'difficult genius' in the workplace and society to hide their almost universal incompetence in all endeavours other than being devious. They make a point of looking busy and acting as if they were vital to the organisational engine, but it is all a façade.

As previously mentioned, I have come to the conclusion that all psychopaths contain a series, or cluster of absolute primary and relative secondary traits. All psychopaths have these five absolute primary traits without exception. Many have most of the secondary relative traits.

PRIMARY ABSOLUTE PSYCHOPATHIC TRAITS

NO REMORSE
Lack of emotional depth in terms of others' problems or hurt. Cheap apology at most. Usually no apology at all. The psychopath will never acknowledge or sincerely apologise for the harm and

misery that they have caused to others. They don't get why they even should.

INVENTED PERSONAS TO MANIPULATE OTHERS

Psychopaths are a different version of themselves for every person they interact with. They also have 'group personas' for family, organisational and workplace interaction. If unexpectedly approached, or taken by surprise due to an unforeseen encounter/chance meeting/sudden waking, the psychopath will often look at partners, friends, workmates and even their own family members as if they do not recognise them. Victims often report being 'scanned' up and down by the confused psychopaths for a brief moment, before the psychopath recognises the person they are looking at. The scanning action buys time for the psychopath to alter their 'persona-approach,' to custom-tailor a new way to approach a situation where they feel they have suddenly been 'put on the spot.' There is also a several-second lag-time when the psychopath 'persona switches' to access the correct version of themselves of which you are being subjected to, even if you happen to be the spouse they wake up next to in the morning. Eyes frantically studying the person's face while they present a forced smile is *very* commonly reported.

USING PITY TO MANIPULATE AND ENTRAP VICTIMS

Kindness and the ability to feel pity are considered weaknesses by the psychopath, rather than noble attributes, and through 'pity plays' they often beckon their target to become unknowingly entangled in their web of lies and deceit.

A MYSTERIOUS OR CRYPTIC PAST

Inconsistent time-lines and missing past histories. Moving from state to state, or region to region under suspicious or vague circumstances — usually without any or little prior announcement. They want to know about your every move and life story, while their own remains elusive or vague. Often has few or no photos of themselves before they met you. This could be due to them having been in prison or to even having been a different gender in the past. Often they were not the war hero they claimed to be without medals they purchased on eBay or Photoshopped images. More likely, they will have an entire multi-layered psychopathic past lifestyle which may include using aliases, prostitution, periods of ad hoc homosexuality, multiple relationships, extremely promiscuous sexual history, several marriages and abandoned spouses and/or children which they want to keep swept under the rug and hidden there.

HIGH TESTOSTERONE LEVELS
(EXTREMELY SIGNIFICANT IN FEMALE PSYCHOPATHS)

Highly impulsive and highly spontaneous sex drive/sexually aggressive/'pervy' behaviour. Upper body strength and pronounced Adam's Apple in female psychopaths. Early baldness in males.

If you know someone who has all of the above primary traits, you are dealing with a psychopath. It does not matter if they have none of the secondary traits listed below, they are still pure psychopath.

SECONDARY RELATIVE PSYCHOPATHIC TRAITS

Sexual Promiscuity/Asexuality/One Night Stands

Narcissism/Boastfulness and a Sense of Being Born for a Special Purpose

History of Brief or Failed Relationships Ending Badly which are *Always the Fault of the Other Party* — wants to, or does, get engaged or married on impulse.

As soon as a relationship is legitimised, the psychopath begins the downgrading phase of piecemeal deterioration, devaluing the spouse while still hanging around to be enabled. Female psychopaths will often get immediately pregnant, or fake or overplay a medical condition as a kind of insurance to keep a roof over their head. The spouse represents a purely utilitarian device to the psychopath. These marriages always end in disaster for the non-psychopathic person caught within such unions.

Camera Persona(s)
First recognised with the advent of custodial police mug shots dur-

ing the late Victorian era. Psychopathic criminals would distort their faces, or tightly close their eyes as a photograph was being taken. This facial contortion was in order to attempt to make them look unrecognisable and to appear to be someone else — the instinctual, knee-jerk reaction by the psychopaths being photographed in order to try and fool this new technology and attempting to create a *camera persona* during their feral 'fight or flight' state while under arrest. In the modern context, the psychopathic camera persona is now implemented by using fake modelling/actor headshots, or actual photos of the psychopath taken up to a decade previously to deceive people looking at the psychopath's social networking or on-line dating service profiles.

Waking up in a Pool of Sweat even in Cold Weather
Falling Asleep Instantly and/or Waking up Instantly
Psychopaths do not have that moment of internal reflection with their inner thoughts at the end of the day. They sleep and wake instantly, similar to a machine turning on and off.

Idealisation Followed by Cold Rejection
At the height of their idealisation of you, the psychopath will show you obsessive 'love,' care and attention. When you have asthma they profess they would give you their lungs if they could. When you have a toothache they will swear revenge on the sugar you consumed in the past. However, once they feel they have you where they want you — or the relationship has ended — if you collapsed in front of them on the street they would simply step over you as if they'd never met you and continue on their way. Outrageous smear campaigns against the discarded victims to falsely portray them as psychologically unstable, self-serving liars, pathetically lovesick, alcoholics, thieves, or abusers are often undertaken by psychopaths following the ending of a relationship.

Eyes Dead and Lifeless
No 'crow's feet' well into middle age due to smiling with their teeth and not their eyes. This is also from not forming a consistent social

identity over the course of their lives. Most psychopaths also demonstrate a predatory, dead/piercing stare — especially when they are annoyed or not getting their way. Their eyes tend to race frantically from side to side when pulling off a scam.

Needing, at Most, 4-5 Hours Sleep a Night

Many psychopaths use sleeping aids, prescriptions and alcohol to extend their sleeping periods in order to deal with boredom.

Faking Cancer or Other Serious Illness

In order to cultivate pity, time-off of jobs, deflecting possible legal action, or more likely to obtain money from sympathetic people, psychopaths will sometimes pretend they have cancer or other serious illnesses. Shaving their heads, eyebrows and body hair to fool people that they are on chemotherapy is not uncommon. Often they disappear for a while for some 'special treatment' overseas. Psychopaths will set up charities and fund-raising events to collect money for their non-existent medical expenses. They can also be known to 'die' while away being treated, only to use this to begin a new identity. Life insurance scams are also part of this strategy.

Does not Dream, or Fabricates Unrealistic Dream Stories

Anyone in a long-term relationship with a psychopath will often remark that they generally cannot recall the psychopath waking in the morning and discussing a dream they had during the night. Psychopaths only seem to dream as very young children and their dreams have a tendency to be intense with vivid recollections of floating — similar to reports of out-of-body experiences. When approaching puberty, the psychopath stops dreaming completely. If an adult psychopath does talk about dreaming it can sound faked, embellished, flowery and unrealistic, such as the dream progressing like a movie — devoid of allegory, metaphor and archetypal motifs. They are making their dream stories up in order to convince their target of some kismet or special bond which the fabricated dream identified. However, after the initial idealisation stage, the victims report never hearing the psychopath talk about having dreams again. Modern research has identified that dream activity during sleep is most active in the frontal lobes of the human brain. Dream imagery and visions are due to complex cognitive processes in and around the frontal areas of the brain. The frontal lobe is also associated with reasoning, planning, parts of speech, emotions, and problem solving — other attributes usually deficient in many psychopaths.

Constantly Looking and Acting Busy for no Apparent Reason

In a workplace setting, the psychopath will move the same empty box or file between endless locations all day long and for no apparent reason. A performance of constant endeavours/project involvement will be projected to others around them. In a corporate setting this allows the psychopath to infiltrate and monitor various departments in order to target potential victims. This also serves to create an illusion of the psychopath being important and vital, when in fact they are simply covering up their incompetence and lack of value to the organisation. An unemployed psychopath will be driving here and there for interviews, meetings, visits and jobs which do not exist.

Highly Unreliable/Broken Promises

Psychopaths will make the most incredibly ambitious plans including you as their right hand man or woman then, on a whim, discard those plans and move on to some other crusade that excludes you. Victims often alter their own life plans to help the psychopath reach their imaginary goals, resulting in appalling emotional, psychological and financial chaos for the victims when the psychopath moves on. Often, these fake plans involve starting a family and raising children. This becomes a dream for the victim and they will move vast distances to new locations, including changing countries, only to find it was a scam when they arrive or when the psychopath pulls out of the deal at the last moment.

Constantly Trying to Correct Others' Opinions (Arrogant Pseudo-Sceptic/Debunker)

Righteous indignation/condescending/always right — never wrong

Crocodile Tears and Unconvincing Emotional Responses, Superficial Laughter

Extreme and Obvious Flattery, Emulating and Sycophantic Behaviour

Lovebombing — designed to release large amounts of dopamine and norepinephrine, while reducing low activity in serotonin within the victim's brain so that the victim becomes emotionally dependent on the psychopath and thus becomes highly vulnerable to the psychopath's suggestions. The areas of the brain that produce dopamine become hyperactive, and are directly related to addictions. Since their teens, psychopaths have learned to manipulate their victims through this technique. The term *lovebombing* was brought into common usage by the psychologist Professor Margaret Singer in her book *Cults in Our Midst.*

Word Salad

Using complex phrases and verbal confusion to make them seem wise and learned in the eyes of others. When you really analyse what the psychopath is pontificating, they are actually saying nothing meaningful or original. This is very common with the academic and intelligentsia-style psychopath. They will also use technical and matter-of-fact terminology during periods of heightened emotional energy. For instance, when their victim is in extreme emotional distress the psychopath will talk about the issue using almost technical language.

Claims to be the Only Person who Really Relates to you

You and me against the world... including socially isolating victims away from family, friends and the community. It is one of the most common methods used to control victims.

Obsessed with the Latest Pharmaceuticals/Hypochondriac

Psychopaths always seem to be taking medication(s) of some form or other, in many cases to deal with STDs such as Herpes. Migraine medications are very commonly used by psychopaths.

Has no Real Creative Talent (Can only Copy – Can't Innovate or be Original)

Can learn to play guitar, or develop a craft even to a high level of proficiency from how-to books, but incapable of developing their own creative vision or individual style. Very often this ability is used to con others into believing the psychopath has a sensitive artistic soul. They never get past that initial adolescent phase where a person wants to be rewarded for what he or she is rather than for what he or she does.

Phoney Altruism

Buys into either secular and non-secular belief systems to appear superior or enlightened. Will align themselves with 'morally popular' causes to make themselves appear enlightened and with a sense of deep moral wisdom and compassion. Includes environmentalism, gay and lesbian issues, abortion, child and animal welfare. But it is always a pose; the psychopath's association with these causes is a veneer to fool others into trusting them. It's always fake; always an agenda.

Easily Takes Offence

Psychopaths will take deep offence at even the most innocuous comment. A harmless off-the-cuff remark taken the wrong way, will be seen as a full-on verbal assault against the psychopath. More disturbingly, they will catalogue to the nth degree every detail of how they were slighted by you for later retrieval from their vast database of personal grudges. The psychopath will produce this event, citing the outrage/hurt it caused — even if the victim has no memory of the alleged insult. Conversely, if the psychopath hurts you, is purposely malicious, or causes offence, insult or injury, the victim is expected to 'get over themselves' and 'stop being such a drama queen' or will be accused of 'having no sense of humour'. A very common statement made by psychopaths in these situations

will be, *"You take things too personally..."* Psychopaths are the ultimate hypocrites.

Gifts Designed to 'Buy You' or to Mould you in a Certain way

Their taste in clothes, the music they think you should be listening
to, the pop psychology books they think you should read.

Little or no Interest in Parenting...

...while claiming to adore their children. Popular phrases include
clichés like, *"I love my children more than life itself."*

Easily Bored

This results in either promiscuity, multiple and simultaneous Internet 'romances', alcoholism and/or drug abuse to alleviate the
boredom.

Becomes Obsessed with a Hobby, Cause, or Individual and then Loses Interest Instantly

Feels they are Entitled to the Best of Everything and Expects to be Indulged

Exploits Friends, Parents, the Elderly or Handicapped

Money, free rent, altering wills, will even fake common mental illnesses to get into psychiatric hospitals, care homes or dependency
clinics in order to avoid paying rent.

Claims to have a Special Relationship with God or Fakes Being Religious (Spiritual Narcissism) or Extreme Atheist

Either extreme atheist or 'Holy Roller.' It's also very common for
psychopaths to mock people who are on their own spiritual journey or reading metaphysical books, and so on.

Expelled/Flunks out from Educational Institutions and then Blames the Entire Institution and not Themselves

While seeing themselves as the highly-strung 'genius' or middle-
aged student (*who never graduates*) psychopaths will arrogantly

parade themselves as intellectuals regardless of their lack of quali-
fications.

Claims to be a Spy, Assassin, Falsely-Discredited Government Scientist with a New Identity, Special Forces Personnel or other Clandestine Agent

Bogus medals, collections of books on certain military campaigns
they claimed to have been involved with — in actuality they are
merely research materials/props they keep around to lend credibility. Will even wear uniforms or medals in public even though
they served no time in the armed forces.

WAKE UP AND LISTEN YOUR INNER VOICE.

Trusting one's instinct is something we all need to become more familiar with when dealing with psychopaths. We have our intuition
for a reason and anyone who has ever been caught in the labyrinth
of the psychopath will always comment later on the many red flags
that were waving. Unfortunately, most people will turn a blind eye
to these warning signs while accepting the psychopath's excuse or
diversion designed to put you off the scent.

A friend told me once about going into a hospital with a psychopath whose father had just been diagnosed with a terminal illness.
Rushing to the hospital, they entered the reception area. The psychopath paused and then turned to my friend and casually asked,
"How should I behave in front of my family? Is there a system to
be followed to deal with this kind of event?" My friend said he was
absolutely dumbstruck. It was such a surreal question to be asked.
At the time, my friend put it down to the psychopath simply being
in shock upon hearing the news.

Then, noticing that my friend was amazed by the statement, the
psychopath glibly continued. "Oh, my family are so dysfunctional!"
According to my friend, the psychopath's family were perfectly normal. They were crying and supporting their sick relative and each
other. He told me he observed how the psychopath looked at them,
took tips from their body language, and then went around hugging
them in the most superficial and forced manner. The psychopath

simply had no idea how to deal with grief for the simple fact that he was *incapable of feeling grief*. The psychopath had no previous experience of profound inner sadness to study and emulate when required. Presumably he will be more prepared next time. Perhaps he even went home and practiced in the mirror.

It is not unusual for psychopaths in relationships to constantly quiz you about what your interests, desires and what your sexual fantasises are. They are constantly learning and evaluating, simultaneously looking for your triggers and perfecting their own techniques of emulating human responses.

THE ICE BREAKING TECHNIQUE

One of the main tactics a psychopath uses to win the trust of even the most intelligent and intuitive people is what I have come to term the *ice breaking technique*. At first it seems very close to the *pity play technique*, but it works on a more specific and targeted level. Politicians and sleazy salespeople (same thing when you think about it) cannot function without the Ice Breaking Technique.

Whereas the pity play technique is used to get them out of trouble/responsibility, psychopaths use the Ice Breaking Technique to lure you into a trap by playing on some issue in your life — or most often your natural human kindness which they see as a weakness to be exploited. They will make sure you are well aware that they *love* their families, friends, dogs and children, and you will be given as convincing a performance as their current skill level allows in order to convince you. Politicians love to be seen and photographed holding and kissing babies and walking their dogs.

But it goes much more deeply and is far more pernicious than just fake image promotion. In terms of verbal and personal interactions, language and carefully-crafted statements and 'opinions' become the weapon of choice for the preying psychopath in 'target mode'.

A psychopath will make sure to have the right books in their hand when they are meeting potential targets. Carrying around a Carl Sagan book to imply they are scientifically-minded when they haven't got a clue what the book states beyond quickly skimming the introduction, or having only read the captions under the illustrations. They could carry a Deepak Chopra book to imply they are a soulful, insightful person, when they are actually dead and cold inside. I can recall laughing to myself when — right on queue — just about every 'enlightened' psychopath I knew could be seen carrying a copy of *The Audacity of Hope* by Barack Obama in early 2007. Whatever the psychopath thinks the target requires, these 'props' will be casually and subliminally displayed leading up to and during the Ice Breaking Technique.

The ice breaking technique will be implemented once they get to know you fairly well and have researched your soft spots and interests. For instance, an on-line psychopathic predator will take an interest in you on a message board or forum and examine in the most microscopic, exhaustive and detailed level everything and anything you post on the Internet. They will trawl these info-nuggets in order to get personal details about you which you may have made public and possibly even have forgotten about. If you let it slip that you volunteer for, say, an African charity, the psychopath who is targeting you will then perhaps sponsor a family in Africa who are in need, and then make sure the psychopath's name is clearly visible as the charity giver on the website. So when the psychopath starts emailing you to begin the hunt, they'll casually mention that they are donating to African causes too… Despite your gasp of surprise — *Oh wow, we are so alike!* — faith hasn't brought you and the psychopath together, *fraud has.*

This is just one example of how fantastically devious they are. Remember, they have no love, compassion, empathy, remorse or conscience inside them, so they fill this void with their predatory, multi-layered scams and Machiavellian plots. It works on every possible level, and covers all aspects of human behaviour and social interactions. They are not a proper human consciousness themselves, but they have studied our humanity in the same way that botanists spend their lives studying plants.

They analyse your every comment and implement pre-scripted and highly-developed scenarios whereby you will hear back from the psychopath everything you would like to hear and then believe you have encountered a true soul-mate or honest politician who — this time — will not be like the last con artist… except you haven't found anything special at all. You're just the latest fish to be hooked on their line.

OTHER EXAMPLES OF PSYCHOPATHIC ICE BREAKING TECHNIQUES:

"Oh your wife died of cancer… how sad. My boyfriend too. I held him in my arms as he died… I know how you feel… "

"My husband/wife slept around on me. I can't understand why. I like sex so much…"

"The environment is important to me. I can't understand people who question man-made climate change… "

"Like you, I also spent months caring for my sick uncle before he died."

You get the idea. Chances are there may be some truth to their stories, but it is always a highly-edited and self-serving version of what really happened.

Here would be the most likely real scenario behind the above statements:

"I heard that some guy I had a one-night stand with years ago and never saw again afterwards died of cancer".

"I cheated on my husband first and he was so emasculated by what happened and upset he could not sexually perform with me knowing other men had been 'in there'. He ended up sleeping with another woman to try and deal with the heartbreak. Matters not, as I was fucking his best friend a couple of times a week."

"I noticed you drive a hybrid and have a WWF bumper sticker…"

"I heard he was dying. Hadn't seen him since I was a kid, showed up at the end to try and get into his will and steal his stuff while he wasn't looking."

WE WANT INFORMATION

Psychopaths, from the promiscuous seducer to the ones with real power, are completely obsessed with monitoring and controlling others in order to pull off their scams while maintaining and cultivating absolute psychological and emotional dependency within their victims. The key to this is their ability to gather information and then to say what the victim wants to hear. This is what psychologists term *interactive linguistic alignment*, which means people sharing the same views bond more closely.

The psychopath is not stating views in which they personally believe, they are pretending to have the same interests and viewpoints as the victim in order to *cultivate an artificial bond*. Brain scans performed by Princeton University neuroscientists of a speaker and listener showed their neural activity locking and aligning in similar patterns during conversations. The stronger their shared viewpoints and opinions, the closer was the coupling.

JENNY'S STORY

"Looking back I am very hard on myself now for falling for his sob stories and the 'poor me' act. He would make it sound as if his story—of 'his absent psychopath father' was 'unique' from mine—when it wasn't at all given the fact it was the same father! Yes he was my half-brother and he became the missing 'father figure' I longed for as a little girl when he came into my life. Perhaps this is one of the most difficult things to accept after dealing with a psychopath—the feeling of having been 'fooled.'

I wanted to know his past. So much time to catch up on, and how I wanted to hear about his adventures and life story. He told me he went to art school—then told me he had not picked up a pencil or paintbrush in his twenty years of marriage. This made me feel terrible, so I went and bought him all the art supplies he would need. I told him he needed to create, as these are the things that feed our soul. However, I found him copying things out of books that he claimed to do on his own. He said he could play guitar and owned one, but didn't even know how to tune it. On and on went the over-inflation of his abilities in everything and anything. He had no soul either.

I am not a 'tattoo' sort of person, but he presented me with a necklace when we first met, of a Celtic heart or love knot. He had the same symbol tattooed on the middle of his back after giving it to me and so while he was having it done. I decided to have it tattooed on me as well since I watched him go though the pain of it. At the time, I felt he was the person who made everything 'right' in my life. My best friend. Finally a family of my own. Lately it feels as if I am 'branded' like cattle to him when I look at the tattoo. Soon after he branded me, he tried to sexually assault me—his own half-sister.

After what my half-brother did to me physically and I was emotionally devastated by the experience, I found photos of him on Facebook, out having fun at parties, laughing, smirking, drinking. Only TWO DAYS after he violated me and I felt like such a fool. Forgiving him almost immediately after the event because he presented an act of sobbing and being 'sorry' and how he wanted to die because of it. It confused me, and I felt numb. But then to later see these photos of him out having a good time while I was still suffering—it was tremendous insult to injury. I hated him. The last time I heard of him all he sent was a photo with a picture of the word GOODBYE written in the sand. No understanding or comprehension of the magnitude of his assault on me. No remorse and no shame."

Jenny's story highlights the ability of the psychopath to become the missing pieces in one's life. In this case, Jenny's missing father figure when she was growing up, the completion of her childhood dreams, and fulfilment of the whole family she longed for as a child. The incident with the tattoo is particularly insightful and disturbing. He was testing her physical and sexual boundaries with this ritual. Jenny could not comprehend that her own half-brother would use this as a stepping stone to a full-blown sexual assault on her. As with all psychopaths there are no sexual limits. Incest is not a taboo to the psychopath — just an opportunity. Fortunately for Jenny she prevented this from taking place.

An attractive half-sister is just another target for conquest. Jenny's trauma is then compounded by discovering images of the jovial psychopath continuing on without a care in the world in the immediate wake of attempting to sexually assault his own half-sister.

So Sad About 'Us'

This is all too common with people coming out of relationships with psychopaths. They'll be fed stories by the psychopath of how they were 'crying themselves to sleep every night' — only to accidentally stumble upon Facebook and Flickr images of the psychopath in their new persona — very often with their new target/enabler — enjoying their new performance during the period they claimed to have been mourning the end of their relationship with you. The pathetic photo in the farewell message in the sand brings home the inability of the psychopath to even convincingly fake heartfelt sincerity — assuming that such 'greeting card' type sentiments are just as meaningful as real emotions. This is due to the psychopath not having the faintest idea what real emotions are to begin with.

Too Much Information

As we move deeper into a society in which personal privacy is being increasingly infringed upon, the psychopath's job becomes so much easier. We have been conditioned to no longer think of our home as a private sanctuary, thanks to endless celebrity magazines and television programmes which film and photograph inside the tacky bling-filled homes of the rich and famous.

TV programmes such as *Big Brother* featuring round-the-clock cameras on the contestant or the staggering numbers of CCTV cameras currently filling our towns and cities by the day are testament to this post-privacy society being foisted upon us by agenda-driven psychopathic elites who want to know our every move and then tell us it is 'cool' and 'hip' for your life to be an open (Face) book.

We are constantly being conditioned by stories of cats being saved from death after having been dumped into a rubbish bin on CCTV and by the rise of the transhumanism movement, which sees humans as obsolete machines to be replaced with 'improved models'. The psychopathic society is in nearly full control now. The elite claim this constant monitoring of you is to better and more efficiently 'protect you,' in the same way you wake up in the middle of the night and catch your psychopath boyfriend going through your handbag and he explains it away as 'for your own good'.

Josef Fritzl told Austrian police during the investigation against him that he chose Elisabeth as his favourite daughter and built a bunker just for her. He felt that he had to lock her up because he was a responsible parent concerned that she was about to become involved with drugs. When his daughter was 18, Fritzl lured her into an elaborate cellar he had built under his home during the Cold War in the late 1970s, with the help of a government grant available for constructing domestic shelters against nuclear fallout. He drugged his daughter with ether and handcuffed her to a wall in the cellar. During the first years he is alleged to have 'kept her like an animal'. Guantanamo Bay, anyone?

The Josef Fritzl rationalisation is typical of the psychopathic mind. He utilised a microscopic fragment of the truth concerning drug abuse, when in fact he used drugs to coerce and restrain her. Contrast this with the politicians who are 'protecting us' from terrorists when in many well-documented cases the same politicians funded the 'terrorist organisations' to begin with. The psychopathic justification — regardless of the bigger picture or impact on others — works just as well with an Austrian incest-obsessed psychopath as it does with Donald Rumsfeld selling Saddam Hussein the same chemical and biological weapons which later became the justification for NATO to kill over a million Iraqis during an illegal invasion.

Most of us are not even aware this is going on, and we take the proclamations concerning increased security and intrusion into our personal lives as being 'good for us.' How did humans ever survive in the past without all this security and control? While we become absorbed in the latest episodes of *Dancing with the Stars* and *Sex and the City*, our phone calls were monitored, our rubbish bins were being examined, and our naked bodies were being leered at by slack-jawed halfwits on airport security monitors.

Services such as Rapleaf store and sell every type of possible data about all of us, gathered from various public databases and by tracking our movements around the web via social networking sites.

It is no longer only celebrities who are followed by services such as JustSpotted.com — an application which provides real-time encounters with celebrities 'in the wild.' When Gawker.com came out with its Gawker Stalker tool in 2006, there was superficial pundit revulsion at the invasion of privacy it represented. Now it is accepted as 'just the way things are.' Google CEO Eric Schmidt told an interviewer that if people don't like the fact that the company is recording pictures of their homes via its Street View cars, *"[They] can just move."*

To Mars, presumably.

Due mainly to the Internet demolishing personal privacy, there has never been a better time to be a psychopath than now. Not only are the pickings easier due to people being apathetic towards their own personal privacy, but acceptance of psychopathic behaviour is becoming the norm. Endless 'entertainment' about insatiable vampires (allegorical psychopaths), shallow superficial female role models who replace meaningful relationships with material consumer products and cheap sexual encounters as a symbol of their 'feminine empowerment,' increasingly violent video games where your child can assume the role of hero who gains extra points by having sex with a prostitute and then killing her to get his money back, the absolute reality we must come to accept is that Western society is now very much psychopathic and being engineered to be this way completely in the future.

The psychopathic elite are patient. They think in terms of generations. They are willing to breed out people with actual discernment, healthy instincts and self-esteem, and focus exclusively upon making round-the-clock privacy invasion 'the new normal' for generations just now being born. It is vital to begin to discover and reclaim your own mental and emotional health and to teach your children to establish their own connection with the greater parts of themselves, because I guarantee that psychopathic corporate interests and the governments they dictate to aren't going to do it for us. In fact, they tirelessly seek to keep us all in denial by, for example, distracting us with episodes of the latest 'reality' show or 'awards' ceremony.

Enough already. It is time for all of us to recapture our humanity and put the psychopath out of business by becoming aware of the pathology and the staggeringly oppressive impact it has on our lives from a personal to a social level. We are all in the darkest corner of the labyrinth of the psychopath. Now let's begin finding a way out.

France has more need of me than I have need of France.   Napoleon

CHAPTER THREE
ALONE IN THE DARKNESS

The point comes in a personal relationship with a psychopath, regardless of whether you have been discarded or are still together, or if you are caught in the clutches or aftermath of a psychopathic control grid structure such as a terrible boss making your life a living hell, where escape becomes the only option. You have to get on with your life. But first you are allowed to be angry and emotionally devastated. You, unlike the psychopath, are only human.

You will be filled with anger and resentment, not to mention dealing with colossal personal humiliation. How could you have loved that person so deeply, and apparently been loved in return, only to discover that your relationship was just another spasm of entertainment for them before moving on to the next dummy? Perhaps you gave your effort and time to support a politician who promised to protect the local cancer treatment centre, only to discover he was drafting the bill which was fast-tracking its closure. Maybe you watched him hold the hands of women on chemotherapy, telling them he would fight for their cause if re-elected. Perhaps you have lived the pain and heartbreak of finding out that your own grandson — your flesh and blood — had been draining your retirement account and signing the deeds of your house over to himself.

You ask yourself — how is the psychopath, now the ex-lover or lying unethical politician or no-good grandson dealing with their cold-blooded ways, while you are deep in torment and personal anguish?

Answer: *They will be doing just fine.*

We have all seen the CEOs of investment banks pay themselves massive bonus packages while public money is being used to bail out the mess they created. They look absolutely chipper and relaxed on TV when the morality of such decisions are put to them. *"What's the problem?"* they blithely say. They are entitled to a twenty-million dollar bonus and can't understand your issue with this. Their cronies in government drafted the legislation to bail them out and pay their bonus packages … *"Take it up with the politicians,"* they say, *"You elected them, didn't you?"*

You hear terms such as *Quantitative Easing* — classic psychopath word salad in the context of political/business lingo for *We are going to use public money to bail out the bankers and you the taxpayers will fund this through your increased personal taxation. Suckers.*

The unfortunate reality is you are never going to get even with a psychopath. It does not work like that. You will only be embarking on a futile meander into the land of frustration and further bewilderment. It could even lead to your death. You must get out of the labyrinth. You have to move on.

It may seem difficult. It may even seem impossible at times, but it will ultimately benefit you more than just about any other experience life can offer in terms of claiming personal responsibility (not culpability; they are two entirely different things.) The psychopath has deleted you from their life as casually as if they had exchanged the batteries in their flashlight. That's how much you matter to them, so why make it worse for yourself? More than anything else, your obsession with justice over their betrayal will just be a humorous sideline for them. They will savour the energy they can suck while watching you suffer. They feed on your attention. In whatever form it comes, they will gobble it up as further proof of their power.

If the psychopath wants to maintain an open link to you as in, *"We can still be friends, of course…'* or, *"It would break my heart if I never heard from you again…"* (bringing a whole new meaning to the term *irony*, by the way) it will be because there is something about you which they might find useful again at a later stage in case their new scam fails. Keeping you in place, compliant to their demands, is a handy reserve fallback plan for them.

It could be your penis, your vagina, your possible money or fame or they may simply need you some day to bail them out of trouble, but it won't be because they have some deep emotional feelings for you. They never had these feelings to begin with. They want you as a *possibly valuable tool for the future.*

MOVING ON AND MOVING OUT

The healing will take time but you'll come out the other side a wiser and a stronger person. Keep reminding yourself that psychopaths are only at most about four percent of the population. I also firmly believe that if you are aware and accept that your lost 'love' or former political hero or two-faced co-worker was a psychopath, you will never attract these monsters into your life ever again. It's almost like you give off an unconscious signal that you are no longer easy prey for them.

Many people in personal relationships with psychopaths attest to this almost psychic quality many of them seem to possess. Victims will hear nothing of the psychopath for a long time. They gradually heal the wounds they sustained, and one day reach the point where they truly feel they have their life back together again and then — seemingly out of the blue — the psychopath attempts to get back in touch, professing their love, friendship or comradeship once again. This has been reported to me by several people, who stated beyond doubt that only via an almost psychic ability could the psychopath have known they were in love with someone new, or enjoying a new life or career or personal success. The psychopath and the victim have even been on opposite sides of the world in some cases when this happened.

FORGIVE YOURSELF

Imagine you have a hole inside you where other humans tell you your heart and soul is supposed to be. Imagine that attempting to make sense of compassion and empathy is like trying to decode some foreign language. Imagine going through your entire life completely void of any of the feelings others claim to experience when describing poetry or love songs or seeing a rainbow or a great painting, and then realise this:

The only way a psychopath can convince themselves they actually exist is by observing the reactions they evoke in others.

Where you and I experience love and joy and sorrow, playfulness and compassion and true creativity, the only thing the psychopath has available to them is endlessly refining their ability to manipulate the emotions of others — sucking the life-force out of one person, then discarding them like an empty husk and moving on to the next. If a psychopath does experience a feeling, it is probably something close to hunger — an aching and endless hunger for something they can never accurately name. It's up to you not wind up as an item on their menu.

Always remember that you are everything these psychopaths can never be. You possess all the emotional gifts and creative loving intelligence they will never have. This is why you must UNLOVE them as soon as you can and very importantly; DO NOT HATE them, either. Accept that you can never 'fix them.' You can never love them or heal them into wholeness. Do not hate them, but do not fall into the trap of thinking you can save them, either. You can never save anyone who does not want to be saved. Any attempt to do so will simply be more ego-feeding energy to them. They want it all — love *or* hate. After a certain point, they simply want your reaction — any reaction will do — in order to ascertain their existence.

To make the beast go away you must starve it into oblivion and decay. But that is only the beginning — you must then take a good look at what you may have felt was lacking in your own life that they sniffed out and zeroed-in on.

A common emotional energy-sucking tactic a psychopath uses at the end of the relationship is to state to the person they deliberately devastated is, *"I'm so glad you don't hate me..."* This is because they are baiting you to scream out something like *"I do fucking hate you! You completely broke my heart!!!"* Ignore this tactic. Even if you do want to scream this out, don't if you can help it.

You are pure loving consciousness with a level of awareness the psychopath can never attain — always know this. Do not be angry at yourself for being a victim. They preyed on you because you were everything they could never be. Inform and educate others about psychopaths and how they operate. Being unable to hide and stalk among us is the only thing psychopaths fear.

One of the reasons psychopaths do not like to associate with other psychopaths (but will if they have to) is because psychopaths are instinctively wise to other psychopaths. They can spot each other across a crowded street. People in relationships with psychopaths often remark that they would sometimes see strangers looking at the psychopath in a curious and odd manner. Later, after the relationship ended and they became knowledgeable about psychopathy, the victims realised that these oddly-staring strangers were other psychopaths checking out the competition.

Keep your Mouth Shut (for a while)

If there is one piece of advice I would give all victims of psychopaths, especially in the early days, it is this: do not under any circumstances *publicly announce your pain and grief in such a way that the psychopath will know it is you talking about them.* I cannot stress this enough:

Don't openly talk about how you feel, online or elsewhere, using your real name or in such a way that the psychopath knows it is you talking about the psychopath.

They could be following your Facebook, Twitter or blog pages in order to get a rush from the emotional devastation you are trying to express. This is just more of your energy for them to feed on. They are pure ego, and enjoy being the centre of attention. As stated in the secondary Relative Traits list, the psychopath will also use this as proof *you* are stalking *them* and have always been the one who was nuts, irrational, or 'losing it.' The psychopath will play that angle with anyone who will listen, to destroy your reputation and credibility with your friends and workmates.

Do not write a song about your pain so the psychopath knows it is them you are singing about. Do not create any kind of art relating to how they hurt you, and then show it to them indirectly. Keep these vital healing processes to yourself, otherwise you are simply gushing out the emotional energy they crave. You are not going to make them remorseful, have a change of heart or feel bad. They do not care about your feelings.

This is one of the reasons I am very much against victim impact statements being read out in court upon sentencing of criminals. Do courts actually believe that a victim of a psychopathic paedophile priest traumatically recalling their abuse while the old pervert sits in the dock is somehow 'punishing' the priest with guilt and remorse? It is nothing less than a nice pornographic trip down memory lane for Father McPsycho, and he is *loving every moment of it.* He joined the priesthood in the first place because it allowed him to rape children with the indirect blessing of the church fathers who would simply move him on to the next parish for fresh meat.

Private journals — write things down, then tear them up or post about it highly anonymously on the net in a way the psychopath will not know it is *you*. Openly talking to someone else can sometimes be the same as talking to the psychopath. Even worse, because now there is one other person (the individual you spoke to) for the psychopath to get attention from — and how they relish this. Find a way to help yourself without giving the psychopath more of what they crave (you are strong enough alone — you don't need somebody else). *Starve the beast!* These psychological and emotional parasites are needier than hell. Don't give them anything they might require from you after they are done with you — especially the attention they so desperately crave.

All psychopaths live by their own rules; they bully, play victim, create drama, and suck the life out of everyone they come into contact with. We all know several people like this, whether we know this about them or not depends upon how well they hide what they really are behind the façade they present to the world. They can at times appear to be the most charismatic, convincing people in the world and only their previous victims know them for who they truly are. They can also elicit a kind of primal fear, something that goes straight past the conscious thought process and aimed straight at the subliminal or unconscious depths of our being.

In terms of real technical, creative and cognitive expression, psychopaths may be mostly imbeciles. They may be terrible at passing educational exams, they maybe without a moral compass and so on, but do not allow your guard down when encountering and dealing with psychopaths — they are the most potent, destructive force in all mankind.

They are in all walks of life and they have no real views or sense of conviction on anything external to themselves except for the emotional response their actions evoke in their victims. In politics, they become Liberals or Conservatives depending on what they want to gain and who they can use to get it. Psychopaths have no allegiance to anything except their own need.

EVIL IS NOT JUST A FOUR-LETTER WORD

Tragically for potential victims of psychopaths, the concept of the pure, social predator evil in others is a major stumbling block. There are those who refuse to believe that evil exists, instead claiming that all things are relative; what may be evil to one person is not to another and both views are valid. I believe this to be a dangerous fallacy that will lead to victims developing magical thinking whereby if they refuse to accept the evil of their abusers for what it is, then perhaps in time it will go away and the psychopath's fake persona will turn out to be real after all.

Then there are those who believe that evil exists, but know that they have been sheltered from it. Such people may even consider themselves fortunate. Then there are those who believe that evil exists and that they have experienced it directly, either through being a victim, or perhaps just witnessing it second-hand. However, what the majority of these people experience is just mundane evil; mundane animosities, mundane jealousies, violence with mundane motivations. Even some really horrible acts are the results of mundane evil.

But there is another kind of cold, calculating, casual psychopathic evil which only certain targeted people are directly familiar with and most of these are first-hand victims of psychopaths. It is something so dark, so alien to their own empathic human nature and to what they had formerly thought could not possibly exist. Upon their first encounter of this cold, calculating, casual psychopathic evil, they are astonished.

As a result, they are initially diminished by the evil psychopathic encounter. There is a loss of innocence so profound that it seems almost irreparable.

This is a problem, for in order to defeat this evil you must be able to recognise it for what it is — you must be able to *truly know it,* and to know it, a part of you must die.

That part of you that dies is necessary for you to move on and get out of the labyrinth of the psychopath. To hope and to pray for the destruction of this evil is all fine and well, but so long as no 'divine' intervention comes, it will never be resolved. The cold, calculating, casual psychopath entered your life as your soul mate, or the home-wrecker who married your father and destroyed everything he worked for, or the predators who — for the most part — rule this planet. The game is rigged for it to be this way.

DETOXING

How many of you reading this — perhaps following the break up of your psychopathic relationship — suffered severe withdrawal symptoms? Perhaps you felt like you were recovering from a drug addiction. It was so much more than just heartbreak — you felt hollowed-out inside. Or you had explosions of intense adrenaline rushes suddenly coursing through your system, waking you up out of a restless sleep and into terror.

You have been dumped by other people in the past and it did not feel like this. You were sad for a while, but eventually you came to terms with the closing dynamics of the relationship in that the other person just wanted to move on; you were very sad, but you got over it in time. Perhaps you saw that the person who dumped you was also genuinely upset about the break-up, too. You may even have remained friends and perhaps a part of you both still loved each other, just not in 'that way' anymore. Life is complicated and we deal with it.

The ending of a relationship with a psychopath is very, very different. You feel as though you had been emotionally raped and discarded, bewildered and utterly psychologically disorientated in the aftermath. You would have been the last person to have ever considered suicide before you encountered the psychopath, but now in your deepest, darkest moments you have wished you were dead. You can't understand why you feel this strongly devastated. You may be a beautiful woman or a handsome man who could find another lover with no problem. However, you feel as if nobody will ever truly love you or know you again.

It changes your entire sense of self. You are torn between wanting to hate the psychopath and wanting to hold them tightly in your arms, or perhaps even just fall at their feet and grovel apologetically for not being perfect. You forget to eat. You catch a glimpse at yourself in the mirror and wonder who it is looking back at you.

You cannot believe how addicted to this person you have become. It's hard to remember the person you were before the psychopath swept you off your feet. In many ways your present sense of self had been cultivated by the psychopath who then just switched you off and took away everything you thought you were. You do not know how to get back to the person you were and have no clear vision of how to move forward into the person you want to be.

You cannot believe how casually they had replaced you for another person, or even nobody in particular — you were so easily disposable to them. They put the blame completely on you and you fell for it. They showed no more emotional depth than if they had changed a TV channel. Yet this was the person who told you everything you wanted to hear, knew your hopes, fears and wishes inside-out and promised to make all the problems of your past vanish.

You were convinced it was 'two souls forever intertwined until the end of the universe.' They made you feel, beyond a shadow of a doubt, that they were that one missing piece of the jigsaw puzzle you longed for since childhood. But it was all a deception.

They said, *I love you* with no more emotional depth than if they had ordered a cheeseburger. They put the wedding ring on your finger and it was just 'playing the game' for them. Then, when they had all they could drain from you, they casually walked away as though you never existed.

You wanted answers. *What kind of person behaves like this? Why do I still want sex from this cold-blooded person? Why does a tiny fragment of me want them back knowing them for what they truly are, and knowing they would destroy me again without hesitation?*

In a 1956 article for *Scientific American* entitled, *Pleasure Centers in the Brain*, physiologist James Olds described how a rat kept without food for a day was tempted down a ramp by a highly nutritious lure. En route to the meal, the rat would receive a pleasurable electric shock. The rat ignored the food, choosing instead to delight in the arousal. Morten L. Kringelbach, author of the book *The Pleasure Center*, cautioned that highly-arousing experiences may consist of impulses exclusively corresponding to 'wanting' and 'desiring'.

This is not the same thing as loving and bonding, hence why in the early stages of a relationship a psychopath makes seduction and sexual excitement a central aspect of the developing romance. You will be told constantly how the psychopath cannot stop thinking about your body; your hair, your penis, vagina or breasts, and so on. They are lying, of course, but it infuses a notion within the current target's mind that the psychopath really does crave them with an intensity of feeling they never experienced for another human. With this endless lovebombing, the illusion of intense emotional bonding reinforces a reluctance to examine the real situation. Soon, the target becomes like the rat in Olds' experiment, denying higher cognitive assessment of the situation — as well as their own mental and physical health — in favour of arousal.

THE FIVE ABSOLUTE PSYCHOPATHIC TRAITS IN ACTION

The pity play/sob stories make you feel nurturing and protective towards them — psychopaths are a target-specific predator. They only hunt for empathic and nurturing people in the same manner certain animals can only eat a particular food source.

Common examples:

Female Psychopath: helpless and hurt damsel-in-distress-type who needs a prince as the world has been unkind to her…

Male Psychopath: little boy lost routine — needs a caring mother-type to make it all better again…

The invented persona was crafted after they researched you and discovered your inner desires and psychological needs. You got what you always wanted from them, even though you may not have directly asked for it. The psychopath read you like a book and implemented their plan of action: the one-size-fits-all solution to the ghosts in your soul. They would even go as far as emulating the people who damaged you as a child in order to 'undo' that past trauma you experienced.

The psychopath's missing past history was so you would never find out that you were not the 'special one' after all. There were many other suckers who were also the 'special one,' all given the same routine by the psychopath before, during and after their relationship with you.

The lack of remorse upon devastating you with their cold, casual or even joyful rejection, was to shock you into wanting answers from them for the incredible hurt they caused you. The psychopath knew these unsettled matters would be an open line back to you if they needed to use you again. Knowing you would always want answers, closure, the final word. They have had *their* closure and the ideal situation for them is to keep you on the shelf in case they ever need you in future. All you ever were or ever could be to them is *a tool*. They set the hammer down, they pick up a screwdriver. That does not mean they won't come looking for the hammer again, especially if the hammer stays right where they left it.

And finally, you longed for them physically because **you got addicted to the sexually-charged 'glow' from the high testosterone levels produced by all psychopaths.** That is the drug for which you are now going cold turkey.

This is how the Five Absolute Psychopathic Traits were used to 'work you,' and why you ended up so badly damaged by the experience. The psychopath found your weak spots, fooled you into believing they would fix them for you, and then made you addicted to them. You were never their soul mate; you were moulded into their doppelganger.

In some ways, victims of psychopaths can be accused of taking part in a kind of unwitting idolatry, whereby the victim worships the bespoke persona, rather than the hidden predator underneath. We see this constantly in politics where voters become infatuated with certain cult-of-personality-style politicians who are little more than actors reading a speech written by highly-paid spin doctors.

Al Gore knows as much about Climate Science as Paris Hilton, but with enough slick graphics, neuro-linguistic programming (NLP), aided by grovelling journalists who question nothing and enhanced by the camera cutting to star-struck Young Democrats in the hand-picked audience, even intelligent people will fall for this kind of corporate and globalist propaganda being passed off as science. Not to mention the number of people who will believe every word that comes out of Gore's mouth for no other reason than that he is not the overtly repugnant Skull and Bones frat brat George W. Bush. The current psychopathic control grid version of politics becomes completely ridiculous once you see it for what it really is.

The good news is that increasing numbers of people are seeing this consensus-trance of devious political agendas and manufactured politically-affiliated fake duality for what it is.

The days of *I am a Democrat (Republican, Liberal, Conservative, Socialist, Tory, Labour, Green Party, etc)* are coming to an end. The scam is up and the psychopathic control grid which has fed us this circus for decades knows it. Hence the panic-driven rush towards transhumanism and posthumanism.

Robots — unlike disgruntled voters — question nothing and do as they are told until they have served their purpose and are decommissioned and dumped on the scrap heap. How very psychopathic indeed.

The psychopath is the human psychological version of the great white shark. It is ruthlessly efficient in targeting and devouring its prey, but that is not a sustainable lifestyle and eventually the messy past becomes too big. It's tiring to keep up a persona. Even actors have time when the cameras are not running, when they can drop the character they are portraying for a while. The psychopath gets sloppy, blurs their lies, forgets details. To squeeze the last bit of 'high' out of their time with you, they may go for more and more outrageous lies and fantastical claims. They may become more controlling or abusive.

Eventually, though, they get bored or tired or just ready for something new. You may begin to question them and the things they do or say, and they overreact, trying to make it seem as though there is some deficiency in *you* for doubting *them*. At this point the projection technique will become centre-stage.

The psychopath will already have either found, or are deep into researching, their next potential target. You will notice them become suddenly interested in topics and subjects which they previously had no particular interest in, and seemingly completely out of the blue. The psychopath may join a gym, work out, lose weight, change their hairstyles and the way they dress around this point. They are building their new persona to work their next target.

The psychopath will then start projecting their own agenda onto you, implying it is *you* who is cheating on *them,* or claiming you are becoming close again with your previous partner. Victims are confused and bewildered at these groundless accusations. Once this happens, the devaluation of you is unstoppable and you will be unceremoniously discarded by the psychopath within days or weeks. You have served your purpose.

Psychopaths only like the beginnings of things, and this movie they have scripted, produced and starred in with you is over. They move on to the next project, starring them and a cast of new victims. However, the mode of operation results in a messy social legacy for the psychopath, and the accumulation of past victims germinates the seeds of a bitter harvest every psychopath is doomed to reap eventually.

As the 1940's American entertainer and comic Jimmy Durante insightfully said, "Be nice to those you meet on the way up, because you will meet them on the way down." The psychopath eventually falls without anyone below to catch them before they hit rock bottom.

TESTOSTERONE

Elevated levels of the male hormone testosterone in both male and female psychopaths is a very distinct marker in assisting with positive identification of a psychopath. This is not to say that anyone who has high testosterone levels — especially women — are psychopaths. We must retain emotional neutrality at all times when we begin to consider if we are dealing with a potential psychopath or not.

For example, an aggressive or impulsive woman may be suffering from a condition such as Polycystic Ovary Syndrome and as a result could be subject to hormonal impulses which can result in negative behaviour. They must have the other four of the five absolute traits (no remorse, invented persona, using pity and strange or contradictory life stories), before you can determine you may be dealing with a psychopath. One swallow does not a summer make.

However, a high level of testosterone present in an individual — male or female, can be very useful towards making a positive ID of a psychopath, in the same way the great white shark has a very specific dorsal fin visible above the water to help us identify the presence of that predator.

Many other traits underlying psychopathy are triggered by high testosterone levels. This would include fearless impulsiveness, sexual impulsiveness, and other traits listed below. According to well-validated research, psychopathic females have a greater over-all 'dose' or genetic load than most male psychopaths have. This has been supported by data showing that there is also a greater risk for the offspring of female psychopaths (compared to the offspring of male psychopaths) being born with a higher genetic load of testosterone, with the result that these children might (according to some studies) have a much higher incidence of inherited psychopathy. Psychopathic women are also more likely to give birth to male children.

Researcher and sociology and human development professor Alan Booth at Penn State in the USA suggests that men who have high testosterone levels are also likely to experience frequent episodes of unemployment and troubled relationships, broken marriages and strained relations with their children. They may find it difficult to remain in a monogamous relationship and could suffer from a higher risk of sexually transmitted diseases. There is also a tendency to gamble and to take risks which may result in financial and legal difficulties, as well as physical injuries due to an impulsive, boisterous nature. This could generally be applied to all men with high testosterone levels, though we can see the classic male psychopathic archetype standing out clearly within Booth's overall description.

Other physical traits of males who have high testosterone levels includes a ring finger longer than an index finger, a receding hair line, heavy growth of facial and body hair, acne, and high cheekbones with a low brow ridge. The abundance of testosterone in male psychopaths may also explain the 'glow' many victims speak of.

High testosterone levels in female psychopaths can lead to virilisation; increased muscle mass, redistribution of body fat, high metabolism, enlargement of the clitoris, severe migraines, deepening of the voice, pronounced Adam's Apple, and increased perspiration even during cold weather. It is also important to note that most psychopathic women with high testosterone levels are not necessarily 'butch' or manly — but they are rarely elegant and 'ladylike,' either. Often, their posture can be unfeminine when viewed from behind, in terms of straightened arms and lifted shoulders when they walk.

The high testosterone also feeds the hyper-sexual aspect of male and female psychopaths whereby their sexual stamina/adventurousness and intensity leaves a deep psychological impact on victims. This takes the form of the 'hot sex' novelty aspect of the courtship phase, though once the relationship is established the victim finds the sex life then becomes robotic, often violent, generally emotionally unsatisfying and loveless. In many cases it vanishes fairly quickly. The 'lovemaking' ends when the psychopath has gotten a firm emotional and psychological grip on the victim's consciousness. Generally, this is also when the psychopath begins having sex with other people, with multiple simultaneous affairs not being uncommon. This can happen within weeks and in some cases days of being married to the victim.

AMYGDALA

Even if the underlying cause(s) of psychopathy remain elusive thus far, one absolute certainty is the role of the amygdala located deep within the limbic part of the brain. The amygdalae are a cluster of nuclei inside the medial temporal lobes, vital to how humans process emotional reactions, including the storage of emotionally-charged events. Brain-imaging studies have demonstrated that the amygdala is activated when most people even consider the possibility of indulging in morally questionable activities.

Memories of emotional experiences which elicit fear behaviour within the central nucleus of the amygdalae have been shown to be muted and even absent in psychopaths. The amygdala is also recognised as the 'fear detector' part of the brain and this may also explain why psychopaths show little or no fear during dangerous and intense situations, including casually lying while under oath, as well as having the ability to pass lie detector tests. Science has still to fully determine why it is that the amygdala is less active in brains of psychopaths, though it is the best indicator thus far in a neuroscientific sense to explain why they do not have the same level of 'feelings' the rest of us take for granted.

AUTISM AND THE PSYCHOPATH

There is an interesting correlation between autism and psychopathy which has not yet been fully researched, nor can it be properly quantified beyond speculation at the present time. Nevertheless, there are many crossover behaviours relating to both conditions which suggest that in terms of neurological conditioning, further research into the relationship between both disorders may be worthy of serious attention. Considering how similar both states are, I have often wondered if psychopathy is autism gone malignant, as in, if autistic people are the 'positives', are psychopaths the 'negatives'?

According to Alison Gunson, founder of the Narcissistic Sociopath (Survivor Support Group) on Facebook and with more than 30 years experience working in the UK mental health field, *"Whilst there may well be a link between autism and psychopathy as 'the Id' (the existential worlds) of both are so self absorbing — we all know autistic people do not manipulate whereas a psychopath is the master. Autistics do not perceive or need 'enablers', a psychopath can not exist without them."*

People who have lived with psychopaths for long periods of time have noticed they demonstrate many of the same traits found in autistic individuals. These can include:

COMPULSIVE BEHAVIOUR

In a psychopathic sense this can manifest as extreme adherence to rules and rituals which the psychopath will have implemented and will expect others around them to also abide by to the letter.

SAMENESS

Psychopaths who have purposely locked themselves into a system not only resist any attempt to modify the system, they will actively prevent others from doing so. This is because the psychopath has invested a lot of time and energy into locking down their victim into a particular state of psychological and emotional dependency. The psychopath will become distressed and angry if the victim begins to follow a new path in life. It is very common for psychopaths to imply to others in a relationship with them that, *'as long as you do not change, I will still love you'*.

RESTRICTED BEHAVIOUR

The psychopath sees no reason to take an interest in matters and subjects beyond the scope of what their machinations require. They only need to know what it takes to keep a particular scam going. Psychopaths have no natural sense of inquisitiveness or wonderment; every aspect of their existence is on a need-to-know basis.

HIGH LEVELS OF PERCEPTION AND ATTENTION

The psychopath is the ultimate student of the human condition. They have no other choice if they are to survive in society, while utilising their unique insight into the potential victim's psychological and emotional needs in order to learn how to 'work them' more effectively.

UNUSUAL EATING HABITS

Psychopaths often have strange and unusual diets ranging from the most complex dietary routines to almost 'scavenger-style' diets whereby the psychopath will eat anything edible at any time just to gain nutrition — behaviour which often drives their partners/ enablers crazy in an effort to cope.

PERSONA SWITCHING

In the 1979 film *Alien*, there is a scene where the crew of the spaceship rewire the severed head of an android they attacked and decapitated. When the head comes back to life again on the table it twitches and looks around before its recognition software kicks in. It then runs a certain script programmed into it.

Anyone who has lived with a psychopath for a long time will have noticed something similar when the psychopath appears to have momentary glitches in their persona-switching where they need a second or two to realise who you are, and what persona program you are being subjected to. Consider the following story sent to me by a woman who lives in New York:

TERRI'S STORY

"In 2007 I was in my fifth year of my marriage to a psychopath. At the time I had no idea he was a psychopath. He was perfectly loving and in many ways the ideal husband. Apart from him occasionally vanishing for several hours now and again to 'de-stress,' (he worked long hours and was away from home a lot) his behavior was mostly charming and considerate towards me. His odd traits I put down to him just being 'quirky' like all people are in one way or another.

Being a professional florist and flower arranger I've always had a lifelong dream of going to the Chelsea Flower Show in London. I have a sister who lives in Scotland and I decided to take a month-long vacation while over there in the UK. When I got back from the vacation and exited the immigration area at JFK Airport there was some kind of renovation happening and I was directed, along with the other passengers coming from London, out through a side entrance. This meant I was not going to walk out through the usual Arrivals areas where friends and family normally wait to greet their loved ones.

So I come into the Arrivals Hall and I see my husband standing there waiting for me with all the other friends and family members at the usual greeting area. He was looking towards the gate to see me come through it eventually. I came up behind him and tapped him merrily on the back of the shoulder. He turned around and what happened next I will never forget. He looked at me for at least two seconds up and down almost like a reptile, shark or an insect studies an object in cold examination before his entire face changed to a huge smile and he hugged me.

I was left very unsettled by the experience. How did the man whom I had lived with for the past five years not know who I was?! I had not changed my appearance at all. More than the initial shock at his strange behavior was how he almost 'switched' into my husband from being someone else.

We are divorced now and I have since discovered he was in 'loving' relationships with three other women at the same time he was married to me. He even had a child with one of them. At first, I assumed he had multiple personality issues, but later I found out about relationship psychopaths and he fit the bill in every way.

Aside from the heartbreak and hurt I still endure, more than anything else, I feel deeply humiliated at just how clueless and trusting I was of him. His psychopathic life-style was extreme, and the world of lies and deception he had built up was completely oblivious to me at the time. He constantly used pity all during our courtship and I fell for it all. Even though he and I had sex almost every night we were married, his pity tactic for other women was that I refused him sex and I had slept around on him!

When I confronted him about his behavior, he tried to blame it on me. We had no major marriage difficulties as far as I was concerned at the time all this was going on. He was constantly declaring his love for me at the time he was doing the same with at least three other women I know of. All the others also believed they were the only woman in his life! It just went on and on. The last time I heard from him, he was being investigated by the state of New Jersey for defrauding an elderly widow out of her home and life savings by assuming the role of a 'carer'.

The one piece of advice I would give to anyone who suspects they are in a relationship with a psychopath would be;

A) if they are always playing the pity card, keep tabs, and,

B) look for any weird behavior which is not normal in most people.

These little things become so important when you finally realize later on what you were dealing with."

The above incident where the psychopathic husband did not immediately recognise his wife is fairly common. There is a delay, a '*lag-time*' in turning on the 'software' in their brains which they play as a specific simulation for you and you only. Remember, a psychopath in your life is only operating a bespoke persona designed specifically to 'work' each individual victim according to their needs and insecurities.

While scanning a person they should instantly recognise, the confused and startled psychopath is not unlike an old cassette music player when one removes one tape, then puts in another and presses the play button. The vacant, bewildered stare the psychopath presents for a few seconds is akin to the time between music tapes when there is nothing in the cassette player to play. When we catch them by surprise, or wake them unexpectedly, it is akin to the psychopath looking for the tape of your favourite music in a box full of albums — a greatest hits of their many bespoke personas which they call upon to manipulate their victims, all perfectly catalogued and indexed, however, when you catch them unexpectedly you can witness the process of actually fumbling for 'your song.'

Psychopaths, even the most skilled manipulators, still need time to get each customised persona slotted into place. Hence the non-husband state which Terri's predator was in for a few seconds. This is due to the bizarrely-functioning electrical system in their brains whereby psychopaths have to *really work at pretending to be normal humans*. They are not 'unwell,' they just have not perfected operating a human body the same way a fully-conscious, fully-functioning, fully-feeling human can do naturally and with ease.

PROJECTION

This term describes the projection, by psychopaths, of their own faults, inabilities and self-destructive behaviour onto someone else. The reasons for projection are varied and complex, and even several volumes would not be able to cover all the ways in which psychopaths in the home, in the workplace and as the movers and shakers of society utilise this technique.

Broadly speaking, projection can be used to highlight and magnify negative or perceived negative traits in victims as a method of destroying the personality/psychological security of the other person, or to deflect attention away from the psychopath's own faults. For instance, a psychopathic female walking into a room full of people might blurt out to her friend — who may be more attractive and stylish than the psychopath — *"I never realised you had an overbite before ... oh, and I love your earrings!"*

The pathology of projection can be used by a psychopathic father who is deeply resentful and jealous of his son by comments like, *"You're nothing like me..."* or, *"You'll never be a great man like me..."* The psychopath is not so much attacking the faults of the victim, as using projection to undermine positive attributes that are perceived as a threat by the psychopath.

The long-term subconscious message the victims receive is that they can never be anything without the approval of the psychopath. The victim is made to feel worthless, helpless and useless at the same time they elevate the psychopath to the level of an infallible god whose opinion is considered beyond question.

One can witness projection all the time in the media, particularly in pieces featuring an 'editorial slant' (the orders given to newspapers by their government and corporate puppeteers) whereby you are fed an agenda in the form of an editorial or 'news story' whose real purpose is to make the reader feel responsible for the perceived ills of society and the world in general. *'We all have to work together to sort this mess out...'* — when it is the politicians and corporations who are the culprits creating 'the mess' in the first place. Psychopaths in personal relationships do this kind of thing all the time. It is also a technique favoured by workplace psychopaths.

WORKPLACE PSYCHOPATHS

As we enter the depths — and debts — of another artificially-engineered global financial recession which will be passed off as a 'natural cycle' once more, the issue of psychopaths in the workplace takes on a more potent sense of urgency. People become concerned about losing their jobs and the impact this can have on them and their families. Psychopaths are acutely aware that this provides them with an opportunity to ramp up their predatory and manipulative advantages in the workplace. Non-psychopathic employees who have to work with or under the psychopath's authority will find themselves having to go extraordinary lengths to tolerate the workplace psychopath's sadistic bullying and ruthless exploitation. The psychopath will always take measures to ensure that if anyone is going to lose their job due to lay-offs, *it won't be them.*

Women in general should be very concerned about being sexually exploited by a psychopath in order to remain in employment. Psychopaths see sex only as a power trip/control mechanism and are sexually neutral in terms of their 'any orifice will do' mindset. Younger male employees may also be victims of sexual harassment by psychopaths who may outwardly project a heterosexual public image with photos of the wife and kids on their desk. They may be asked to 'show their devotion to the company,' so to speak. This is sexual exploitation bordering on rape and employees should be wary of this at all times if they work with a psychopath.

Psychopathic employees and managers are not only in corporate environments, they are in factories, fast food restaurants and retail outlets. They are driving instructors and civil servants, clergymen, physicians and politicians. They all use the sense of economic insecurity to exploit others. They relish recessions as it makes their agenda easier and consolidates their power within the working environment by exploiting the fears of others.

Often, workplace psychopaths are passed off as 'high achievers' or 'difficult but valuable assets' to the employer. Due to their constant boredom and unorthodox sleeping patterns, the workplace psychopath will stay in the office until 3 AM and then be back at the office for a 9 AM meeting with no sign of fatigue. This impresses the boss no end while raising the bar to impossible levels for non-psychopathic employees who feel obliged to emulate these standards.

The reality is that the actual psychopath's productivity and real output never matches the late hours they put in. Often this 'night owl' aspect of the psychopath in the office is to mask the reality that they are incompetent and can't get their normal workload done in an eight-hour workday. Empty offices at night also provide ample time and privacy for looking into other employees' desks, reading their computer files and so on. The reverse rule also applies to the psychopath as most people in the office will often wonder to themselves, *What does Steve do, exactly?*

THE OFFICE PREDATOR

I was in this situation myself back in the mid-90's at a Wall Street investment bank where 'Steve' became the first real psychopath I had ever encountered in a top-level office job in a professional work environment. Steve used to sit at the back of the office with his desk arranged in such a way that his computer monitor was facing the window. As a result, what was on his screen remained invisible to the rest of the office unless someone made the effort to go talk to him whist standing immediately to the side of his desk.

There was always a casual click of the mouse in his right hand as one approached his desk. Neither could anyone in the office figure out what Steve's actual function was in the department in terms of tangible work output. Often, the hand-written documents he produced were sheer gibberish filled with unintelligible scrawl, featuring entirely different handwriting styles from page to page as though *different people had worked on the document.*

Yet he wielded huge influence and power among the other staff. He was 'assigned' the passwords to all other department computers, though his own was never revealed to others. He also removed all the external hard drives from all the other PCs *and locked them in his desk at night.* This created a sense of dependency within the other employees who needed him to access their portable hard drives. This was all done under the guise of 'security and data protection.' He would continually move our desks and cubicles around the department so that when the rest of us returned to the office in the mornings we had to hunt to find the new location of our desks. When we questioned the reasoning behind this confusion, Steve would chalk it up to something called 'Samurai Management', implemented to keep us feeling 'active and less bored.' And yes, you guessed it — his own desk always remained in the same position.

Steve was incredibly glib and superficial, but convincingly charming to most, using this professional 'great guy' performance to endear himself to the department head — an unattractive woman in her thirties. Steve, on the other hand, was tall and good-looking. The two of them often went out drinking in bars after work and he was constantly complimenting her and playing on her insecurities. It became obvious that there was a sexual relationship between them to all who observed their body language while they were together.

One evening, I was completing a project and needed a graphic logo which was on a portable hard drive on Steve's desk. Luckily, he had forgotten to lock it up as he did every other night and I brought the hard drive to my PC to find the logo. What I discovered was thousands of hardcore pornographic images — both gay and heterosexual. Not just a few dozen images, but *thousands* which had been downloaded from USENET pornographic bit servers mainly located in Russia and Asia.

This was in the pre-broadband Internet days when downloading this quantity of image files would have taken a huge amount of time and company bandwidth. This was what Steve was downloading and looking at all day on his PC, and what he closed when people approached his desk. Being worried about losing my job and not wanting to make a fuss, I returned the hard drive filled with porn back to Steve's desk.

Shortly after I moved to another department in the company, I was told that Steve was eventually fired for making a racist comment to a Pakistani manager of the company, telling him to, "Go have a curry and stop bothering me." Recently, I did an Internet search on Steve (he has a very unusual surname) to find out what happened to him in the years since. He is now a manager at a radio station which specialises in 'Gay and Ethnic Minority Programming'. From a social networking site I was able to discover Steve is also now the 'gay partner of the station's advertising manager'. Obviously, his employers at the station have not done a background check on Steve to discover his previous dismissal from a major Wall Street firm for racial abuse of another employee.

The psychopath's chameleon-like nature and persona-switching often allows them to move seamlessly between roles.

My advice to anyone working with a psychopath where you find you cannot easily leave the job: *wait and be patient.* The psychopath will always go that one step too far and be found out. Their high testosterone levels make them impulsive and reckless, and this is always a recipe for self-destruction. Show no fear around the psychopath and never tell them your personal business and what you did on the weekends, or about your hobbies and particularly anything very personally significant, such as your spouse being ill with a serious disease. The psychopath will exploit every possible avenue towards finding that Route 1 to your psychological destruction.

I would also strongly advise against drinking and over-eating to deal with the psychopath after working hours. Take a yoga, meditation or martial-arts course. Natural remedies such as valerian will allow you to get a good night's sleep so you can be as rested and restored as possible to deal with the psychopathic assault when you get to work the next morning. Look after yourself and eventually you will get through this. Hang on to your sanity at all costs.

There is no harm in looking for another job. It gives you something to focus on. You could be surprised how these things pan out once you set your intention in motion.

When people write to me relaying their issues with a workplace psychopath making their lives a misery, I always remind myself and tell them the story of another psychopath I worked with in an Irish company who made my own life very difficult for a time by handing me assignments for both of us to work on (in reality this would be me alone) at 6:30 PM on a Friday evening — just to destroy my weekend while making it look like he was devoted to the company.

After I left the job I by chance bumped into him waiting for my bags at Dublin Airport and he seemed so nerdy and powerless and small — and nothing to me. In the office I was literally terrified of his wrath — along with the 'creepy' energy, manic stare and his passive-aggressive demeanour. Once free from the environment of the office he looked as if I could have knocked him down with a feather.

This small tale serves to illustrate how psychopaths create a feeling of their power, awe and control in others — but it is a spell we are under. Beneath the façade, they are pathetic.

Now you know how the psychopath game works in all aspects of life and society — let's move on.

nothing baffles the schemes of evil people so much as the calm composure of great souls.

Gabriel Mirabeau

CHAPTER FOUR

COVERING YOUR TRAIL

I n his paper, *Intelligence as a Person-Situation Interaction*, Dr Robert Sternberg lists five fallacies of thinking. He states: *"There is another dimension to person-situation interaction: the extent to which particular situations elicit 'stupid' thinking in intelligent people."*

All of his five fallacies range from a sense of godlike indestructibility to extreme hubris, and occur mainly in the context of perceived or actual power and dominance over others. Dr Sternberg is one of many scientists who have discovered that the enjoyment of power and control over other people actually changes brain chemistry and behaviour. Some people are more prone than others to these effects, depending upon personality type along with social and environmental factors. Psychopaths know no other way to live, other than to gain and hold power over others— similar to an addict seeking a drug fix. They are subject to the above fallacies all the time and for the rest of their lives.

One of the most startling aspects and horrors of the psychopath's abrupt departure is how they can literally switch off as though you never existed. To a normal human, this can be completely emotionally devastating. It is bad enough that this person can simply walk away from your long-term relationship, but they can also abandon the children you had with them.

It is next to impossible to express just how emotionally damaging it can be to hear one night that you were, *"... the love of my life, I will die in your arms!"* and then thirty-six hours later not being able to locate them, only to eventually receive a text message or email with the message, *"We're through."*

Perhaps your boss continually took you out to lunch and made statements such as, *"You're my right hand man and you have a great future here…"* and you thanked him by working long hours while telling all and sundry what a great guy he is to work for. Then one day, out of the blue, you come into work one morning and someone else is sitting at your desk. You are shocked, bewildered and confused. Guess who's his 'right hand man' now? Not you, in case you haven't already figured it out.

Likewise, their lack of remorse can seem incomprehensible and alien to us, as can their inability to even understand the emotional carnage they have visited upon their victims.

Having been personally subjected to some of the above situations, I have spent a sizeable portion of my adult life looking for answers to the question, *Why do some people become psychopaths and what makes them behave the way they do?*

I have read everything from psychology and self-help to metaphysical books dealing with the issue of psychopathology, but still they have all fallen short of the explanation my inner self — the auditor of my soul — requires for me to exclaim, *"Yes! That's the answer I was searching for!"*

It was not until the summer of 2009 that a profound insight was born in me, and it was this: **Psychopaths are not human as I understand human beings to be** — they are something very different altogether. I had arrived at the conclusion that a psychopath is a broken, negative consciousness who resides inside a (mostly) normal-looking human body.

Most people's experiences with first-hand abuse at the hand of a psychopath is based on a personal relationship with one. You were unknowingly 'in love' with a psychopath, and the dream you once revelled in with this person suddenly exploded into a visceral nightmare you could hardly bring yourself to accept. You felt as if a giant claw had been thrust into your body and torn out everything that was once in there — including the person you thought you always were. You want to know why this happened, yet you are not even able to clearly define *what exactly has happened.*

Aside from the heartbreak, the initial assumption is that something terrible has happened to your 'beloved', or boss, or business partner, politician, parent or friend. A reaction to some medication they were taking? Perhaps a head trauma? Multiple Personality Disorder? Surely nobody can switch off their feelings and change their personality just like that; there must be a medical reason.

The answer to these questions is *none of the above.* You tragically encountered real Evil in the most literal sense of the word.

Behind the months or years of perfectly-constructed performance by your psychopath is a nothing: a void, a blank, a hunger for something the psychopathic entity can never define.

They now see no further benefit in playing this part and have moved on to a new role — and another decent, kind, loving human being to destroy.

It is next to impossible to grasp how they suddenly show neither affection nor compassion towards you. You are treated to a completely new, cold and emotionless persona. *"Who is this stranger?"* you will ask yourself over and over again. It is so bewildering that you are left with symptoms similar to Post Traumatic Stress Disorder.

This leaves you initially feeling that *you* may have caused the problem.

If you do confront the psychopath and you are 'lucky' enough to get a statement from them, they will 'Gaslight' you — making you question your own version of reality and convince you that you were the one who drove them away. They will do this so effectively that you can end up believing it for a while.

You will not be able to grasp why they do not miss you in return. This is because you were *only a tool to gain what they wanted at the time.* You were a tool and they can always find another hammer or stapler or tin-opener; the world is full of them.

The only reason the psychopath did not kill you is because going prison would be a disruption in their routine, *but if they needed to*

*kill you to get what they want and knew they could get away with it,
they would have done so without a second thought.* This is the main
reason why psychopaths do not usually kill — too much trouble,
too risky and it would take too long to figure out how best to dispose of your corpse and hide the evidence.

They have a new host to feed on now and resent any time taken
from them by any demands from you. You're history now and you'll
be expected to do them a favour by going away (but not completely, as we have seen). If you do not go away, the psychopath can
arrange this for you, but they would really rather not spare the time
or effort. Much easier to assassinate your character rather than your
physical body, though there is no moral issue for them, either way.

The consequence of your disposal — either physical or emotional — is purely a pragmatic question for a psychopath. Most choose
to delete you from their immediate sphere of contacts rather than
rolling your lifeless body up in a blanket and dumping it in the
woods, but make no mistake; *they will do this if they have to.* However, they would be more likely to pay someone to do it for them. Better still, why don't you do them a huge favour and just kill yourself?
Not that they'll ever thank you for the convenience, of course.

Killing yourself would save the psychopath a lot of bother, and
will sometimes bring in a nice insurance payout to be spent on lav-
ish gifts for their next 'useful idiot'. Not to mention it will tie in
nicely with their well-orchestrated smear campaign portraying you
as emotionally unstable and in need of professional help, all playing
in nicely with the campaign to discredit you which the psychopath
launched just prior to the abandonment. *Just business.*

Matters not that they once put a gold band on your finger and
looked into your eyes and swore their marriage vows to you before
your god and everyone else. You're now surplus to requirements
and any past 'performance' on their part shouldn't be taken into
account. Anyway, the psychopath has to move onwards and up-
wards.

In a September 2010 *Esquire* magazine article with Newt Ging-
rich's ex-wife Marianne, she was quoted as saying, *"He believes that*

what he says in public and how he lives doesn't have to be connected."
Old Newt's modus operandi will strike a chord with anyone who
has been in a relationship with a psychopath.

The rules they assign for others — which we have adhered
to — never apply to the psychopath. Before long you are caught up
in their crazy-made world and you find yourself in the position of
believing black is white and white is black.

So here you are wondering how you could have been so gullible,
so clueless and oblivious to this theatre of the absurd? Somehow,
you came to believe beyond any doubt that the shadow puppets on
the wall and the puppet master was one and the same thing. *"Why
me?"* is an expression you will become very familiar with.

THE CHEESE IN THE DEVIL'S MOUSETRAP

The psychopath is nature's supreme psychological predator. Their
place within human society is like a sniper in a watch tower, peering
through their metaphorical scope and waiting for the perfect shot
to line up in the crosshairs. However, the only weapon they need
is your own psychological make-up. An entire arsenal of 'buttons'
is contained within your personality and the psychopath will pick
and choose amongst them in order to gain your devotion and then
reap your soul as they discover which yields to the least pressure.
You never had a father growing up? The psychopath will be your
surrogate daddy. Your sex life with your present partner has gone
stale? The psychopath will be your perfect harlot. Your husband
recently passed away? The psychopath will become the perfect new
parent for those poor, fatherless children left behind. The psychopath will be all these things and more. For a little while.

If you have a need in your life which you are convinced is un-
satisfied the psychopath will become what it takes to fill that gap
with a precision which would make the leading nano-technology
engineers green with envy.

People in the aftermath of a psychopathic relationship always
think back to their first date or initial encounter, and the stories are
almost always identical. The psychopath tended to be somewhat
quiet, not saying much at all except to encourage the victim to spill

everything. The psychopath would smile, then tend to alternate looking at you, then glancing away from in an almost bored manner. What the psychopath was doing was evaluating you as a target and then compiling a database of your wants, needs and desires so they could then begin to cater to these missing pieces within you. They were also lightly testing the waters for control triggers, seeing how you responded if their attention appeared to wander for a moment.

This is also why these psychopathic relationships develop with almost frightening speed. You are not so much swept off your feet as exploded out of your shoes and you barely have time to consider what may be really going on. You have also been targeted because you have a trusting and caring nature. The sob stories and pity plays the psychopath implements in the early stages of the relationship blind you to any pernicious agenda which you are being subjected to. Everything seems to be going amazingly well and incredibly quickly. It is also very exciting and pleasurable to the victim — the 'lovebombing' becomes quickly addictive. The intense sexual energy of the moment is exhilarating. That is why psychopaths so often feel like soul mates in a relationship, or your best friend at work or in an organisation — they project your own persona back to you in their 'assumed,' bespoke personality, the result being you essentially *fall in love with yourself.*

However, as soon as the relationship is established, the downward trajectory from idealisation of their victims and towards the inevitable devaluation and discarding begins in earnest. It may take weeks. It may take months. It often takes years. Nevertheless the psychopath always begins the devaluing of their victims as soon as the relationship is legitimised and is always on the lookout for an 'upgrade' from you to someone who can offer the psychopath whatever they need next.

You will then begin to suspect that the early days of blissful excitement was just a method to make you be their stepping stone to the next dummy. Matters not if the victim is a lover, a best friend, a child or a sworn comrade. When you become obsolete you'll most likely feel things slipping away from you before it officially happens. But — and this is vital to understand — *you will never get confirmation from the psychopath until they are taking the final callous leap to the next stepping stone.* On the contrary, asking what is wrong will only be used as ammo by the psychopath as evidence of your instability.

KAREN'S STORY

"From the moment I met Frank our relationship moved along at unbelievable speed—so fast in fact that looking back I now believe I was not being allowed time to pause and reflect properly upon what was taking place. He reminded me so much of my brothers and now I am starting to wonder if he was mimicking them—knowing how close I was to them and admired them as people. Within three months Frank was literally begging me to marry him. I decided I wanted to live together initially and we moved into our first home. Red flags almost instantly began to show up. The one day he had off a week he spent the entire time sleeping, he would not let me buy the items and furnishings I wanted for the house. Then, upon the eve of deciding that the relationship was not ideal and I should consider leaving, I became pregnant.

I did what I assumed was the right thing and succumbed to his constant proposals of marriage. Our daughter was born and two more children came along within the next nineteen months. I became a mother as rapidly as I became Frank's wife. Everything happened so fast—I was exhausted but was enjoying life as a mother to my children. All during this period he had almost no involvement with me or the children and the incredible promises he made to me during our courtship phase went out the window as if he never made them to begin with.

As my bond with my children became deeper, Frank became a stranger in our home. He wanted no involvement in parenting of his own offspring. He claimed I was nagging him when I requested he take a bigger responsibility in the raising of his own children. He was almost never at home and there was a sense of dread the whole time he was around. He was like a dark cloud of negative energy as soon as he came in the front door. Even when he was sleeping you could still sense it. Then I discovered he had stolen my jewellery while I was in hospital giving birth to our daughter.

Although Frank was working eighty hours a week and self-employed with a seemingly thriving business which invested in expensive and impressive machinery, he brought home next to no money. I later found out he was purchasing property behind my back without me knowing about it. Then I began to uncover that he had been cheating on me with other women literally as soon as he was married to me. In fact, not only was Frank a serial adulterer, he was also a serial home wrecker having destroyed three marriages as a result of him seducing women. Among these was the marriage of his best friend John, whose twenty-five year marriage to Ellen ended after Frank seduced her. Frank showed no remorse and blamed all the issues on everyone else. Frank would spend up to five hours a day on the phone talking to Ellen as a friend when all the time he was working her with a fake sympathetic ear — learning what buttons to push.

As if Frank's serial adultery, stealing, bad business management and compulsive lying wasn't enough, what really amazed me was his relationship to his own children. He had none! Except to consider them a pest and somehow it was all MY FAULT for getting pregnant. He always projected this image of a busy go-getter when in fact he was the most lazy person I have ever known. Then as Frank further distanced himself from our family (except when he needed my business to underwrite his loans) a far more disturbing and sick side of him emerged. He showed the full extent of his depraved and predatory nature.

One night offering to drive my seventy-two year old mother back from the hospital after visiting my father (he never offered this kind of compassionate help before this) Frank tried to seduce my mother in her home. He began French kissing her and she, alone and terrified, threw him off her, screaming. He completely denied it when I confronted him about it claiming my mother lied. He then followed my father around a shopping mall harassing him claiming he was married to a slut! My father who is seventy-three chased Frank out of the mall and Frank ran away terrified! He is a coward when it comes to a man challenging him. I know I should have left him then, but I can honestly say he was able to mind-control me very effectively — not only fake performances of repenting, but also claiming that the children and I would not survive without him. He played on my insecurities non-stop and it really did become a kind of truth for me in a way. Crazy-Making and endless judgment of me to make me feel I was worthless. I actually had come to believe this eventually. I found out later that he was telling everyone that, "Karen is crazy and needs help" and to imply I inherited this insanity from my parents.

Soon after this he offered to look after the kids to show what a devoted father he really wanted to be, and to give me a break — a few days on my own. This was to be his last chance to prove himself. He literally went on a psychopathic rampage as soon as I went out the door. He stole all my valuables, cash, the kids' beds and left the kids on their own to [go and] see his other women. Then it began to unfold that Frank was a paedophile. He began a relationship with a woman behind my back and unlike his own children became in effect a stepfather of sorts for her twelve year-old son and eleven year-old daughter. I have since been told by this woman that while he coached her son's soccer team he made all the boys strip naked, showed them his private parts and then would disappear into a locked bedroom with his new girlfriend's eleven year old daughter often spending the entire night with her. While this took place he started to show an interest in my sister and began sending her text messages of his true love for her!!!!

As his life was in complete turmoil, he went around as if nothing was the matter. He loved to project this boastful windbag, big shot image of himself to anyone he met. Frank claimed to be a brilliant businessman even though this only translated into buying expensive trucks (during a recession) and leaving them parked in the yard for all to see. This was also used to seduce his secretary as in 'all this will be yours one day...' Absolutely nothing bothered him, he had no shame for what he did and ALWAYS deflected the blame for his actions onto others. Including the eleven year-old girl he was with. As a result he got away with everything and made sure that there were no other witnesses who could prove anything against him.

Since I left him he has continued to make my life a misery. He claims to have saved my life one night and I have repaid him by leaving him and breaking his heart. He stated to people, "I should have let that ungrateful bitch Karen die that night and my life would be a lot easier now." He told his lawyers he wants full custody of the children he never showed any interest in. He is an extremely cunning manipulator who can lie without blinking an eyelid. He will not accept any blame for the things he has done and portrays himself as an innocent victim to his family who incidentally believes his every word. There are days I truly believe Frank is demonically possessed—I really do. He isn't human."

Karen's incredibly harrowing tale of Frank's spectacular pathology shows mainly how sex to a psychopath has nothing to do with anything other than controlling and manipulating people for a power rush. From a young girl to an elderly woman, from teenage boys to married women, all are equally desirable to a psychopath in terms of gaining domination over them, while psychologically destroying them for the psychopath's own gain. Psychopaths manipulate people so effectively and in such a short time — Karen's statement that she had 'no time to think' is a very commonly reported experience by people who have had their lives taken and reprogrammed.

Victims' brains are literally rewired by the psychopath. This is why not passing judgement on victims of psychopaths is very important when they start to look for help from counsellors, family and friends. The last thing people like Karen need in this situation is to be told, *'You brought all this on yourself'*. This also demonstrates a real need for some kind of anonymous resource for recent victims of psychopaths such as a hotline number they can call where professionally-trained people or other recovered victims can offer support and advice to recent survivors of psychopaths.

WHAT WAS IT ALL ABOUT, REALLY?

Upon seeking clarity in the aftermath of a psychopathic relationship, the victim then proceeds along the path of recovery by wondering what was in it for the psychopath anyway. Money? Sex? Social status? A wall-size plasma TV? The psychopath always has a relationship with something you supply them with and that is never you as a person — it is something *you have* which the psychopath deems useful to them.

One of the main findings contained within Martha Stout's otherwise excellent *The Sociopath Next Door — The Ruthless vs. the Rest of Us* is her conclusion that psychopaths only want to win. To a point she is correct, but from my own experience I feel that Dr Stout has gotten off the highway one exit too soon. Sure they want to win, but it's a means to an end.

What they really want is the power rush they cull from the emotional energy released by the victims whom they have defeated. This is what they are truly after. That's the real game. All the other trinkets, cash, orgasms and freeloading are just a means to an end. The spasm of excitement knowing they 'nailed it' is the main payoff for the psychopath. But it is just that; a spasm, a rush, a quick thrill — and then it's on to the next scam in another vain attempt to fill this canyon of emptiness within them.

This power and thrill-seeking insatiable appetite makes the psychopath beyond a doubt the single most dangerous and destructive living organism in the history of planet Earth. They have ruthlessly psychologically destroyed and coldly murdered hundreds of millions of human beings throughout history. From the parasitic grandson tampering with their grandmother's medication trying to induce an overdose in order to hurry up collecting their inheritance to the warmongering totalitarian tyrant commanding mass military power and all the levels of psychopathic frequencies in between, their legacy upon this planet has been their on-going creation of a hell on Earth, and they are not finished yet.

THAT INSATIABLE, MALICIOUS VACUUM

Their glorious age is only beginning as a society of proto-psychopaths is being cultivated with frightening speed in media, business and politics. We are being rushed towards the psychopathic technical transhumanist and posthumanist agenda beloved of the most elite psychopaths, hence why we as a society who are not psychopaths need to become wise to this before we become completely extinct. We have no choice.

If there such a thing as a battle of Armageddon then it has already started within the arena of human consciousness. Maybe it is time to stop watching *Dancing with the Stars* and start paying attention to something meaningful for a change.

This is why psychopaths who have become billionaires with all the money, social status and power they ever wanted are still not satisfied. They become captains of industry, then feel the need to become statesmen, opinion-makers and social engineers. They fund military insurgency uprisings and coups in third world countries just because they can. They love to play god, developing their concept of perfect societies where 'useless eaters' will be eliminated in favour of endangered species of rare centipedes and pond moss in remote locations — locations where the human inhabitants are usually dying of disease and starvation.

Psychopaths are never satisfied because all psychopaths have this sense of emptiness inside them and an insatiable hunger to dominate others. Most psychopaths suffer from a level of boredom which is hard for the average person to even comprehend. There is quite literally nothing in there — a psychological and spiritual vacuum which can never be filled and only offset with occasional rushes of power from their 'wins'.

From the impoverished psychopath wastrel living rent-free in their grandparent's house, flicking through the Home Shopping Channel with someone else's credit cards, to the big-time globalist player regularly leaving their palatial mansion in order to attend endless political think-tanks, round table conferences and summits, all psychopaths are always, constantly bored. Controlling, manipulating and then eventually destroying others provides them with distraction from this boredom.

Psychopaths feed on the emotions of others. Not only the emotional carnage and misery they leave in their wake but also feelings of love, devotion or even hatred from their victims. Psychopaths do not know how to be a person because they are not proper humans to begin with. They cannot take pleasure from the company of another human being unless they are manipulating, exploiting, seducing, stealing, emotionally destroying or murdering them. They live absolutely within the feral moment and have no real sense of past or future beyond the results of the present moment's manipulation. It is just one rush to the next, then they become bored and move on to the next individual, charity organisation, social club, committee, family, nation or entire continent to manipulate, exploit and eventually ruin.

Now imagine living your entire life this way. Not getting any real satisfaction from anything. Filling the boredom with devious manipulation, sexual promiscuity and pity plays/sob stories which pay off in an instant rush, only to be immediately forgotten. Such pathological behaviour only leads to self-destruction — isolated in decay, surrounded by no one and nothing meaningful as the psychopath's sphere of manipulation gets smaller and smaller as options decrease with the onset of age and victims in common begin to compare notes.

The answer is this: *there is nothing in it at the end for the psychopath*. They have an itch which can never be scratched. The victims — if they approach the experience correctly — can emerge the real winners in the end.

According to most mental health professionals, nearly one in every twenty-five people in Western society are psychopathic to some degree. If you were constantly targeted by a psychopathic parent, schoolteacher, or bullied as a child or if you were in the military as a young person, your chances of being individually-targeted by psychopaths as an adult are greatly increased.

Mass media, politics, organised religion and television in particular are psychopathic enablers since these institutions have more often than not been created by psychopaths, and they reflect the pathology of control and cold-blooded deceit present in all psychopaths on a macrocosmic level. They have also softened you up and primed you for the everyday psychopath you will meet on the streets, in the bars and during working hours. As above, so below.

DOUBLE STANDARDS IN MEDIA

For all the self-righteous hand-wringing, that *Something must be done!* mentality of crime reporters, newspaper editors and journalists in media, the publications they work for often demonstrate a level of double standards worthy of any psychopath.

An example I ran across recently was published in the *Philadelphia Inquirer* newspaper, in an October 14, 2010 interview with a psychopath killer named Ira Einhorn who is currently serving time for killing his girlfriend, Holly Maddux, then proceeding to live with her corpse in a trunk for 18 months. Her mummified remains were eventually found in Einhorn's apartment in 1979. In the *Inquirer* story, Einhorn gave a classic psychopathic narcissistic gasbag-style interview to journalist Ronnie Polaneczky.

Typical of the psychopathic mind, Einhorn spent most of the interview pontificating about his unsung genius, how he was going to fight for the justice of wrongly-convicted fellow prisoners in between boasting about being a sexual athlete. The journalist did a very good expose on the psychopathic criminal personality, and identified him as such. I then noticed in the upper right hand corner of the *Inquirer's* website next to the headline for the Einhorn interview a link to the history of Philadelphia criminals. Clicking on the link revealed the following text:

"Philadelphia has had a long history of violent or colorful criminals, from Al Capone to Ace Capone to Thomas Capano, from the Arsenic Gang that poisoned or killed 100 people, to Jocelyn Kirsch, the glamor-

ous Drexel student convicted of scamming friends and acquaintances out of more than $100,000 with her beau to finance their high life."

The link provided 110 pages of images relating to various murderers and con artists, many of whom were psychopaths and all portrayed by the newspaper with an almost rustic quaintness and the victims of these killers and con artists entirely overlooked. This link was next to the aforementioned 'outraged' interview of a contemporary psychopath.

We see this over and over again in the media. Editors and other pundits being superficially outraged and conveying with their *'Enough is enough!'* editorialising when reporting on present-day crime. However, in terms of past crimes by psychopaths, these become 'colorful criminals'. The message here is, given enough time, the ruthless, psychopathic Ira Einhorns of today's newspapers become the charming rogues of tomorrow.

This hypocrisy in media is not just limited to violent crime stories. The business pages of many newspapers will be filled with endless tributes to various banking and big business players who will often champion bail-outs by taxpayers while demanding government lay off tampering with big business. The same issue of the same newspaper will often have front page headlines such as, BANKS ARE RIPPING US OFF or WHITE COLLAR CRIMINALS A LAW UNTO THEMSELVES.

Are these publications anti-psychopathic behaviour or do they simply find it colorful? How credible are editorials demanding justice and victim' rights when the same newspapers make superstars out of past psychopaths? To this day, the massive Ted Bundy publicity machine is kept alive by journalists who claim it is what people want to read. Do they really? Or is the media conditioning people to believe they should be continually seeing the Ted Bundys and Al Capones of this world as pop icons?

MOVIE PSYCHOPATHS

The Talented Mr Ripley (1999)
This masterpiece of late 20th century filmmaking is a psychopathic

tour-de-force in terms of Matt Damon's brilliant performance as persona-switching, cold-blooded Tom Ripley.

Set in 1950's post-war Italy, the story involves a working-class young man living in the US (Matt Damon) who is employed by the father of a wealthy shipbuilder to locate his son Dickie Greenleaf (Jude Law). Ripley is ordered to travel to Italy to persuade Dickie to return to home to help run the family business.

Although Tom Ripley has never met Dickie Greenleaf, nor studied at Princeton University, upon his arrival in Italy Ripley contrives a deviously psychopathic encounter with Dickie and his girlfriend, Marge Sherwood (Gwyneth Paltrow), claiming to have been at college with Dickie while pretending to share his obsession with jazz. Although typical of what occurs in so many real-life psychopathic relationships, in this case a concerned friend's intuition, Freddie Miles (Philip Seymour Hoffman), Miles instantly knows that there is something not quite right with Tom and his story.

Ripley — a closeted homosexual — comes to increasingly idealise Greenleaf and his carefree, rich and spoilt lifestyle in Italy. Desperate to be a part of this, he attaches himself like a limpet to Dickie, who has by now grown tired of Ripley's classic sycophantic and obsessive presence. An argument ensues in which Ripley injures Greenleaf. When Dickie fights back, Ripley murders him. To conceal the crime, Ripley sinks a rowboat with Dickie's body still on board, then swims to shore. There is also a suggestion of necrophilia having taken place.

Ripley then begins to steal Dickie's identity — wearing his clothes and assuming his lifestyle in Italy. He uses his typewriter to communicate with Marge, attempting to make her believe that Greenleaf has deserted her. He carefully plans his movements and the sending of messages from location to location around Rome, deviously constructing the illusion that Dickie is still alive.

The Talented Mr Ripley is a superb character study of a psychopath. All the classic traits from persona-switching, idealisation, sexual inappropriateness, jealousy and lack of remorse for his actions. Perhaps the best-made, brilliantly written and acted and beautifully-directed film yet made about the psychopathic condition. Highly recommended.

Another film is *Scarlet Street* (1945). Perhaps the most powerful portrayal of a sexually feral, pity-mongering, manipulative and vicious female psychopath in the history of Hollywood cinema.

Joan Bennett's brilliant portrayal as the remorseless prostitute and swindler Katherine 'Kitty' March in Lower Manhattan during The Great Depression contains all the classic elements of female pathology and how it impacts on a hapless male victim. Edward G. Robinson plays the role of Christopher Cross, the gentle-natured bank cashier who upon leaving an office party held in his honour one night 'rescues' Kitty from being assaulted by her boyfriend/pimp Johnny Prince (Dan Duryea).

Cross, who himself is wedded to a middle-aged psychopath, and who, according to Cross, 'was real sweet before we married,' psychologically bullies him while mocking Cross' desires to become an artist. Within no time Kitty March picks up on the missing and unfulfilled aspect of Christopher Cross' mundane and troubled life and thus begins to become the woman he has always longed for. Not only is Kitty March young and attractive, but she presents herself as his artist's muse. She then begins to ask him for money which he steals from his employer.

The movie contains all the classic elements one expects from a female psychopath. In particular, Edward G. Robinson plays the perfect psychopath's victim in the central motif of the story. The man is quite literally engulfed in a world of psychopaths, all of whom prey upon his basic human decency, unrecognised artistic talent, his miserable home life and his sexual/romantic frustrations.

Kitty — barely encouraged by Johnny's greed — signs her own name to Christopher Cross' paintings and she becomes an art sensation as a result of their forgery. Upon discovering this, Cross is manipulated by Kitty into accepting the situation — robbing himself of the success he has longed for as an artist in order to indulge Kitty's psychopathic agenda. He eventually ends up destroying his life in order to appease Kitty's pity ploys and deceitful machinations.

The moral of the film is centred around the concept that natural justice will take care of psychopaths eventually. Their own pathology is their undoing, as the film's conclusion illustrates. Tormented and broken, Cross is haunted by thoughts of Kitty March, whom he has murdered. This results in Johnny Prince being wrongly sentenced to death for her killing. Cross attempts to hang himself, though survives the suicide attempt.

Destitute, and with no way of claiming credit for his own artistic genius, Cross spends the rest of his life haunted by ghostly voices of Kitty and Johnny together in the afterlife, making love to each other for all eternity. Even after her death, the tragic Cross spends the rest of his life ravaged by guilt and remorse while trying to convince the police he was the real killer and that Johnny was innocent of Kitty's murder.

oh what a tangled web we weave
when first we practise to deceive!
Walter Scott

CHAPTER FIVE

TRANSFORMATION

Nature stirs up biological evolution now and again with mutations and as a result, organisms are forced to adapt to this new mutation in order to survive. I prefer to consider the purpose of psychopaths on this planet as nature's way of making the rest of us adapt to and integrate our personal, social, emotional, psychological and spiritual evolution via contact and interaction with them. Ironic, considering the psychopath's hunger to use and exploit decent people for endless gain and power, that nature may be using them in the position of pawns in a game they have no chance of winning in any meaningful sense. Looking at it this way, psychopaths are ultimately here to serve *us*.

People who have come into contact with psychopaths often claim that they have a reptilian quality about them. A part of the human brain is indeed called the R-Complex; it is our reptilian brain and it is concerned with genetic survival through sexual activity, and is cold and selfishly driven. Fortunately, we also have something non-material within us called *compassion* which overrides this.

Psychopaths have completely different brainwave functions than the rest of us. But they are not 'unwell people'. They know the difference between good and evil and choose evil because it excites them and fills them with a sense of power. If you have no empathy and remorse inside, evil can be very good for business, and for gaining what you want as easily as possible. You simply take it from someone else.

Thus far, I have tended to concentrate on the more negative aspects of the psychopath and their effect on victims. To be a victim of one, either in business, an oppressive personal or social situation, or in a relationship is a horrible, heartbreaking, soul-destroying experience. It can seem as though you are all alone and there is no justice in the world. But take heart; the reason they targeted you is because you were everything they can never be. There is a bigger picture in all this, and embracing this is the beginning of a wiser, stronger and more independent self.

Even though an individual with a psychopathic personality can lead what appears to be — on the surface, anyway — a typical life including jobs, spouses and children, their employment and marriages don't last for long periods of time. Psychopaths' lives are continually on the verge of destruction. Even though they will appear to maintain an air of calm towards others in a given social situation, a large amount of the proverbial poo can be hitting their fan in many other aspects of their lives. They are always dodging or weaving a succession of dilemmas or crises and the people 'closest to' the psychopath are usually completely oblivious to this up until the point the psychopath walks away. At this point, the curtain is pulled back and the truth revealed.

John List murdered his wife, mother and three children in 1971 in order to 'start over.' Before the murders, he pretended to go to work for several months from his home in New Jersey to a job he had been fired from. Even though his life was in chaos, none of this was known to his family members as he maintained a commuter lifestyle to a job that no longer existed. When he could no longer hide his bizarre 'work' routine, and unpaid bills began piling up with no money to cover them, List decided that the best option for him was to kill his entire family and begin a new life with a new identity.

One day, List came home from his pretend job early to shoot his wife in the back of the head and his mother in the eye. His two younger children, Patricia and Frederick, came home from school and he shot both in the back of the head. His eldest son, John Jr. was playing football that day. List made himself a meal, then casually drove to collect his son and take him home, where he then shot his son ten times to make sure he was dead.

John List calmly and matter-of-factly placed the bodies in the basement of his home and left to make a new life for himself on the other side of the country until — thanks to the TV show *America's Most Wanted* — he was arrested in 1989. His new family had no idea either of his past crimes or who he really was.

The ability of the psychopath to sail through all their chaos and causally undertake the most appalling acts, seemingly without a care in the world, could not happen without the psychopath finding very specific sorts of enablers. John List may be the rare example of a psychopathic family killer, but all over the world every day non-violent — male and female — versions of John List walk out on their families and loved ones to start over again. Just business.

They care not one iota that they left others in misery, heartbreak, financial turmoil and psychological ruin. This is why psychopaths spend their entire lives looking for the likes of you and others like you; you are the most glittering prize of all. But as soon as they steal from you, the thrill of the hunt ends for them and they are off to destroy or use someone else. It is an endless cycle which for all their scams and tricks are doomed to fail. They can never fill that 'gap' missing in them. That empty void inside the psychopath was you for a while. So never take being a victim of a psychopath personally — you were one of many who got the same treatment.

There is an interesting correlation between this collection of and conquest of humans and another trait found in many psychopaths (mainly males), and that is their obsessive, short-lived, full-on pursuit of a hobby or interest. For no apparent reason and usually out of the blue, a psychopath may develop a sudden interest in collecting old books or animation art or anything else which takes their fancy. They will then become utterly and completely obsessed with this hobby for a couple of months, draining their (or more likely your) finances and then lose all interest and forget about it as if they never were into it in the first place.

This collecting and discarding of inanimate objects by the psychopath applies equally to their 'collecting' people. To the psychopath, there is simply no difference between collecting commemorative plates or collecting enablers, whether sincere and loving individuals or devoted employees. The psychopath no more sees the people in their lives as being any more emotionally important to them, or worthy of respect, than porn magazines or salt and pepper shakers.

This may seem unbelievable to normal human beings, but it is a reality of psychopathology. Psychopaths see no value in any human being other than their utilitarian usefulness to the psychopath. Consider the following comment by former US Secretary of State, Henry Kissinger, when he stated to Alexander Haig that military men were, "... *dumb, stupid animals to be used...* " as pawns for foreign policy. This failure to grasp the true worth of the human condition coupled with their apathy towards the effects of their life-long manipulation and deceit starts to generate a very messy trail behind the psychopath. The good news is the arrogant, infallible, god complex of the psychopath never considers that it will eventually reap what it sows.

All psychopaths get it in the end. Either at the hands of a judge, or public disgrace and scandal ending with their reputation and/or finances in ruins. More often than not, they end up isolated in decay, surrounded by no one and nothing as their sphere of manipulation gets smaller and smaller and their options decrease with the onset of age. Will this stop them from changing their ways? Not on your life! Until their last breath in a hospital or nursing home they will be scanning and scamming someone nearby.

ENDGAME PSYCHOPATH

So what happens when a psychopath has failed in all their schemes, has no more decent and trusting human souls left to exploit and enslave, or — if we are lucky — is sentenced to many years in jail? For want of a better term, Not-So-Instant-Karma, but karma nonetheless. There is simply no concept of past-actions-leading-to-present-dilemma within the mind of the psychopath. They cannot and will not perform any kind of self-observation because they have no sense of self *beyond the reactions they evoke in others.* They are always in target mode and they are almost exclusively living within the present. It's not that they have no goals — many do — but they are continually making plans on-the-fly to keep up with their hunger.

The consequences of this behaviour and its effect on the people they dispose of so callously is never taken into consideration. Once in hunting mode, the psychopath develops tunnel vision — all that exists is *the now, the hunger* and *the target.*

What all psychopaths are destined to reap from their behaviour over the long term is misery, and will eventually end their lives like an AA battery with no power left. A normal human, with the ability to feel and evolve, to dream and appreciate, create and cherish, to look within and to grow spiritually is akin to a rechargeable battery.

The psychopath on the other hand needs a continual supply of victims in order to re-energise. We can get our emotional energy from the smile on our true love's face in the morning, the deep and sincere joy of the company of our friends and family, or even that nice feeling you get when you help an elderly person put their groceries into their car. None of these would appeal to a psychopath other than a performance as a means to an end — they can never grasp the rich and fulfilling aspect of normal human existence.

Psychopaths — those *Intra-Species Predators* as Dr Robert Hare brilliantly termed them — use their human form as little more than skin-suit-camouflage to prey amongst us, always over-estimating their invincibility and playing that one poker hand too many, forever failing to make any contingency in the event their appeal in the eyes of others will wane — which it always does.

Psychopaths never consider that one day everyone will be sick of the sight of them. They are oblivious to the subtle intricacies of normal human interactions. They can fake almost everything, but not perfectly and certainly not forever. Their one-man or one-woman show is always forced to close due to lack of patrons, but they won't notice until the curtains close in front of them and there is no more applause.

This is their Achilles' Heel in terms of safeguarding their long-term manipulation of others to constantly bail them out. Spouses and family members will often have to resort to explaining to the psychopath how they feel and how others feel who have been damaged by them. This will be done time and time again until the enablers finally give up. They may end up doing this over and over and for many years with no meaningful or tangible outcome in order to get the psychopath to understand how they actually feel. Even the most devoted victims of psychopaths locked into a state of almost Stockholm Syndrome-style imprisonment will eventually have enough and walk away from the psychopath.

Psychopaths neither understand or appreciate the impact their behaviour has on others — even to a certain extent on the psychopath themselves. They cannot come to terms or even begrudgingly accept any weakness, obvious folly, or any kind of personal failing on their part. If something goes wrong it is always someone else's fault regardless of the amount of evidence presented against the psychopath. Not only does this become bewildering to the psychopath's enablers over the long term, they will also become bored with it. A young, attractive psychopath can offer sexual rewards to enablers, but what happens when the psychopath's looks fade and their often legendary sexual stamina loses its intensity? A normal person would have the love and support they had given to others over their lifetime to fall back on. The psychopath never gave this — so there is no reciprocal affection insurance policy for them to collect. The game is up. Even then, the psychopath will admit no failing — it is always someone else's fault and never theirs.

The absurd lengths psychopaths go to in order to deflect any kind of personal responsibility for their pathology can be staggering. Being caught red-handed with an army of credible witness' testimony is still filled with endless grey areas in the mind of a psychopath. There is simply no acknowledgement of guilt, no matter how damning the evidence presented against them.

A friend of mine who worked as a psychologist in a battered women's shelter told me once how during a court case involving a psychopath who broke his wife's nose, he stated in all serious-ness that he did her a favour, as her nose was too big and she was much prettier now thanks to his assault on her. He stated this with a straight face to the prosecution during the trial and expected sympathy from the court as a result.

Psychopaths will lie even when telling the truth would be their best option. They are also infallible in their own minds. As a result of this lack of inner reflection of their own true nature and how it relates to their place in the world at large, there is no personal evo-lution beyond learning how to manipulate others more effectively.

The psychopath always rejects information which may under-mine their glorified image of themselves. Couple this with the highly unstable self-control aspects of a psychopath and they end up being deleted from people's Christmas card lists more then they get onto new ones. Constantly and arrogantly correcting others' opinions and beliefs in a smug, patronising and/or condescend-ing manner, their spiral into oblivion and decay always traces the downward trajectory of the psychopath's existence, a trajectory that only accelerates over time.

Their emotional and psychological development age is essen-tially infantile. As a result of this, their exterior persona is not as rigid as they portray it to be. Something always happens to reveal their inner true nature from behind their social façade and it is al-ways something they perceive as a threat. Their feral, flight-or-fight mindset will often have them responding in the most violent way as an automatic, involuntary response. For instance, nurses and doctors report that some patients receiving an injection will un-expectedly swipe at them to defend the perceived danger — as if they are under attack. I suspect psychopaths make up the bulk of patients in this situation.

Their flight-or-fight response will be seen in situations where a family home is on fire and the psychopathic parent will run out into the street to save themselves before even thinking of calling emergency services to save their spouse and children still inside the house.

This selfish response repeated in varying degrees and across a whole plethora of social interactions sets off people's alarms bells eventually. Psychopaths can also be lawsuit-happy halfwits who take absurd legal action against anyone who annoys them. This will further socially isolate them, as who wants to be around someone apt to drag you into court for the most minor indiscretion.

Along with the psychopath's sob stories/pity-mongering, their tendency to employ gushing flattery as a means of manipulation tends to lose its effectiveness in the end as they lay it on too thick, for too many years. Even the most die-hard compassionate soul, there for the psychopath when they were needed in the past will eventually see it was all an act to con them. Enablers eventually begin to question why every decent lover the psychopath had was 'cheating on them,' or why every job they were fired from was 'unfair dismissal.' Given time, everyone involved realises the psychopath's version of the facts was an immense fabrication wrapped around a microscopic fragment of half-truth.

One skill that some psychopaths have learned to capitalise on is their ability to cook. This is not out of any joy derived from culinary pursuits. They are only too well aware that people nearly always trust someone who feeds them. It is a primal response in all of us to nurture and nourish. The psychopath can often produce elaborate meals and dinner parties and will keep their guests up all night feeding them. However, the 'windbag' nature of the psychopath constantly praising themselves can make the most impressive culinary presentation distasteful after a while.

A SELF-IMPRESSED, SELF-PUBLICIST

How the psychopath loves to pontificate endlessly about his favourite subject — him or herself. All done to a captive audience while the psychopath's hand holds aloft an imaginary baton, conducting his or her out-of-tune invisible orchestra so we can be captivated by their own spectacular glory generously shared with all and sundry. Even past the point where no one is really listening anymore.

Psychopaths can for many years pose as professionals, often as 'consultants,' even when they are not fully qualified to practice any career. There may be some truth in that they spent a year or two in college before they were ejected on the eve of graduation under suspicious circumstances. Not that you'll get the real story. Everyone else at the college was the problem, not the psychopath. Never mind, they will still parade themselves as qualified experts on the verge of accepting the Nobel Prize on any given subject and you'll believe it because they lie so well. For a while. Or until their shoddy work practices and incompetence has someone doing a background check on them.

Psychopaths are either superficial, dynamic 'hotshots' or parasitic wastrels — their hallmark is an incredible ego regardless of their achievements, or lack thereof. Sooner or later, the psychopath will make the mistake of preying on the wrong person, or pushing their scams too far. There is a Bengali proverb which states that *the most placid tiger has the sharpest claws when provoked,* and so the psychopath — the eternal moral and intellectual imbecile and devoid of creative intelligence — always ends up being undermined and demolished by the one they least expect.

Many psychopaths claim to be artists, poets or investigative journalists, 'proving' to their potential victims that they are 'wise, cultured, enlightened or sensitive,' but they could never be real artists, poets or journalists for the simple fact that the only thing they ever create is lies. Without the instruction book or video, they cannot develop their 'art and insight' beyond basic mimicry, but they always believe their mimicry alone is adequate.

Developing an actual skill takes more time than a transient scam requires and they never comprehend that plagiarism is always revealed. They have learned to mimic their art in the same way they have learned to mimic human behaviour. They can read the score, but can never feel the music. They get sloppy and they slip up. People around them begin to realise that something isn't right, and begin to scrutinise the psychopath. The penny then begins to drop...

A LIMITED ENGAGEMENT

There are several studies indicating that psychopaths are completely dependent on observing and emulating people around them so they can get along socially in order to exploit others. Since a psychopath does not have a proper range of emotions, they will put on a show of emotion they believe to be appropriate for the occasion. Sometimes they don't understand the subtle nuances of the delicate social situation they are applying this to and will put on a completely inappropriate display of 'emotion' in the hopes that quantity results in believability.

This overblown performance usually sets off red flags in others. For instance, the psychopath will often behave astonishingly inappropriately at funerals. They will either act apathetic, or pull out the high drama routine in order to prove how distraught they are. They can do incredibly strange things, such as take photos of the coffin being lowered into the grave. They make bizarre requests like asking for a photograph to be taken of them beside the hearse or next to the grave as they knead the soil, never fully realising how weird and insensitive this is to onlookers. They are casting around for authenticity and missing the mark by a mile.

It has also been reported that psychopaths attending funerals will ask grieving widows for a date as soon as their spouse's/partner's coffin is in the grave. Many of these psychopaths would have previously 'befriended' these widows or widowers on cancer victims family support Internet groups upon discovering they were nursing a terminally ill spouse and subsequently attend the funeral in order to 'target' the bereaved, often travelling long distances to show how 'supportive' they are.

Psychopaths will also gatecrash weddings to prey on lonely, single individuals feeling vulnerable during the heightened emotional nuptial atmosphere. Psychopathic females will also purposely portray the 'wallflower without a dancing partner' archetype at weddings and other social engagements in order to target sympathetic males. These psychopathic females will often deliberately attend this function alone, often preventing husbands and boyfriends from accompanying them.

BIOLOGICAL DEVELOPMENT
VERSUS EMOTIONAL DEVELOPMENT

Think of what an infant wants. An infant believes they are the centre of the universe — the universe as the infant knows it, that being: a dry bottom, a comfortable place to sleep, mother's milk and mother's love. An infant deserves that. As one grows, normal people realise that others have needs too. This is called compassion and empathy — an understanding of inter-relationship dynamics.

Psychopaths are completely broken in this regard and have never grown beyond infancy regarding their fellow human beings or anything meaningful to society as a whole.

Their inherent laziness always has them looking for the easy option. Like an infant who has their needs serviced, but who never develops a sense of personal and ethical responsibly as they grow up, the individual psychopath gets married so they do not have to pay rent. Rather than doing the real job of catching criminals, the bureaucratic psychopath assumes everyone is a potential criminal and fills office buildings, schools and entire cities with CCTV cameras. This laziness always results in the psychopath taking their eye off the ball and someone ultimately notices their agenda.

On the other hand, their high levels of testosterone lead to a reckless need to become more and more powerful and influential regardless of consequences. Either for the 'high' they get or out of pernicious laziness or boredom, the psychopath always goes one step too far and gets caught. With this, the entire parasitic lifestyle they have cultivated begins its unstoppable collapse into failure. In the long run, psychopathic individuals, and psychopathic social control mechanisms all have sell-by dates.

PSYCHOPATHS AND SUICIDE

Some psychopaths do in fact commit suicide when the scam is up and all the possible options and safety nets are finally exhausted. They are not killing themselves out of personal anguish, or to end any kind of psychological torture. It is simply time for the psychopath to 'check out'. Often, their suicide notes — if they leave one behind — betray their legendary narcissism right to the very end. An Irish Catholic priest, Fr Sean Fortune, killed himself before he was about to go to trial for the sexual abuse of twenty-nine boys, in some cases having made pornographic movies of the rapes. He titled his suicide letter, 'A Message From Heaven'.

Being evil is not a sustainable option in this world. Psychopaths all fail in the end. From the shifty drifter or promiscuous lover to the sadistic world leader, they all fail. In the end they render themselves the obnoxious old slut, annoying drunk, failed grifter or Skid Row loser. With a sort of twisted justice, their hunger for the glorious legacy they worked so hard to ensure ends in ruins. A friend of mine once beautifully stated, "Psychopathic individuals are like lizards scrambling through a lifelong desert of their own making."

WHEN THE GAME IS FINALLY UP

At times, psychopaths can seem to react with what are essentially proto-emotions and even some primitive form of regret, only this regret is not so much for other people as it is for how the consequences of their ruthless behaviour rebounded upon themselves alone. They simply regret the loss of their freedom, their resources and their options for continual escape and reinvention. This regret never has anything to do with any inner soul-searching the psychopath may undertake to come to terms with the misery they have caused others. That is not even on the cards.

However, even in the midst of the psychopath's darkest hour, they can change in an instant from regretful depression to instant giddy optimism if the possibility of a get-out clause or new prey enters their sights.

A win is a win to a psychopath and they'll gladly take any they can get. This is often seen in court where psychopaths accused of the most horrific crimes will literally express joyful celebrations if they win an appeal — even with the victims and/or families present in the courtroom.

After a 2010 mistrial was declared by Dallas District Judge Gracie Lewis, killer John Wade Adams was spared receiving the death penalty for the murder of Donna Vick in 1997. Upon the verdict he was not going to be executed but instead go back to prison for life, Adams leaned back in his chair in the courtroom and announced to the victim's family, "I won!"

Reactions like the one above can border almost on surrealism, such is the psychopath's lack of guilt coupled with their inability to admit any wrongdoing. Mark Hofmann was a forger of rare documents and a ruthless killer whose victims included members of the highest agencies in the US Government and the Mormon Church. When Hofmann's schemes began to unravel, he constructed bombs to murder two people in Salt Lake City. As he stated in a 1987 interview regarding his forgeries, "It's not so much what is genuine and what isn't as what people believe is genuine. When I forged a document and sold it, I was not cheating the person that I was selling it to because the document would never be detected as being a fraud. Obviously, if I would have known they would someday be detected, I wouldn't have done it. I didn't feel like I was cheating them."

Hoffman's response is as clear an insight into the psychopathic mind as one can get.

We see this kind of twisted, perverse sense of 'logic' in all psychopaths. From the politician who gets caught red-handed taking part in corrupt activities to the relationship-psychopaths rationalising their devious machinations, they will never admit in any direct way a meaningful acknowledgement of guilt.

Often, friends, colleagues, workmates, family members and other individuals still enamoured with the psychopath, and perhaps even in denial of their behaviour, can go to extraordinary lengths to legitimise the psychopath's excuses. On a radio programme regarding former US President Bill Clinton's lying under oath about having sex with Monica Lewinsky, Gore Vidal responded by excusing Clinton's behaviour, declaring that it was not actual vaginal sex with Monica Lewinsky since in Clinton's Southern Baptist culture oral sex is not considered sex as such.

Eventually, the time comes when even the most loyal enablers of any psychopath have had enough. This is because the psychopath never reforms nor comes to terms with the errors of their ways. They will indulge you with endless promises of having finally learned from their mistakes, but it is all lies to shut you up.

In the 1971 cult movie *A Clockwork Orange* there is a depiction of a scientific attempt to reform a psychopath named Alex, played by Malcolm McDowell, by means of behavioural therapy, hopefully resulting in his aversion to sex and violence. Alex indulges his reformers and 'cures' himself of his pathology. His final line in the movie is, *I was cured, alright!* as he vividly anticipates the resumption of his psychopathic lifestyle.

THE LONG GOODBYE

Anyone who has ever been in a relationship with a psychopath would be well aware of the constant empty threats they can often make to leave you, knowing very well that the false sense of dependency which the psychopath has fostered within your subconscious mind will prevent you letting them walk out the door. That carefully-orchestrated moment when the psychopath goes into the bedroom and opens the suitcase and begins packing their clothes, waiting for you to plead, *"Oh no, please don't go. Let's talk about this!"* The victim never sees the smirk upon the psychopath's face as the predictive programming they placed within them pays off in being begged to stay. If this is the situation you are currently in, why not try throwing their suitcase and belongings out onto the street and slamming the door behind them?

When you are in a relationship with a psychopath, there are far worse things than being alone. It is better to be unemployed than remaining in a job where a psychopath — either your boss or co-worker bully — is making your life miserable. There is no point looking for justice from external forces in most cases. The only one who can attain this is you — and you get real justice by reclaiming your personal, psychological and spiritual independence, then walking away and getting on with your life. You are free now and your real transformation to a better you has begun. Living well is the best revenge of all.

IS HE/SHE A PSYCHOPATH?

- Do they fall asleep and wake up instantly — or have strange sleep patterns?
- Do they ever talk about dreaming? If so, do they sound as if they are inventing a bogus fabrication?
- Do they blame every problem in their lives on someone else?
- Do they tend to be boastful and self-praising, despite initially placing you on a much higher pedestal?
- Do they demonstrate unconvincing emotional responses; superficial, forced laughter or crocodile tears?
- Do they constantly proclaim their altruistic nature and charitable deeds, yet these alleged acts always seem to have taken place in the past before you knew them?
- Do they have a superficial surface-level knowledge of just about everything, yet lack any real insightful or expert knowledge into any one particular subject?
- Do they 'read' books very quickly, and if you ask them about the book or novel in detail they can only give a basic synopsis?
- Do they align themselves with belief packages in order to proclaim moral or intellectual superiority?
- Are they intolerant of fringe subjects including alternative issues, spirituality or metaphysical topics or alternative health that you may developed an interest in, but which they fail to understand or have time for? Rather than deal with the fact that your new interest is not for them, along with respecting your desires to follow your own knowledge path, do they instead ridicule and try to reform you away from these topics?
- Do they have vague personal life stories and career paths?
- Do they seem to have done almost nothing with their lives apart from living off other enablers?
- During emotionally-charged situations do they use sex to divert you from the matter at hand?
- Is "make-up" sex a regular occurrence in the relationship?

- Are they always going back to school or college, including taking night courses, but never seem to graduate?
- Do they have a constant supply of 'poor me' stories?
- Has the relationship developed really quickly, especially sexually? Telling your children and pets they 'love them' soon after meeting them?
- Are they constantly quizzing you about your life, interests and want to know your every move?
- In the early days, did they follow your posts on specific Internet message boards, even though they apparently had no interest in this subject matter before they met you?
- Is everything about your life just amazing and perfect to them? Your looks, your abilities, your children are the cutest, most perfect kids, your mind is brilliant, you are an incredible lover of no equal, you have the best taste in everything, etc?
- Do they drink the same beverages you do when you order them and order similar foods and generally use any angle to imply they are just like you in every way?
- Does their persona change when they become intensely angry at a third party and then switch back again?
- Have you ever caught them by off-chance in the street or out in public and you found their body language, demeanour and facial expressions were unlike the ones they used around you?
- Were they initially very quiet on your first date, allowing and encouraging you to do all the talking?
- Do they bring up past incidences, saying things such as, "Do you recall the time when you...?" and you have no recollection of the event?
- Do they always seem to be coming and going constantly or busy for no meaningful reason?
- Have they claimed all their previous relationships ended due exclusively to the faults/abuse/problems/infidelity of the other party?
- Do they mock, ridicule and smear the name, reputations and behaviour of their previous partners?

- Do you ever get the feeling that 'something just isn't right here'—even at times when the relationship seems to be strong and even blissful?
- Can they switch from depression or anger to excitable giddiness instantly?
- Do they want to legitimise the relationship ASAP—move in, get married and have children right away?
- Did they talk about the two of you enjoying old age together soon after you first met them?
- Did the flattery, idealisation, sexual intensity, mimicry and sycophantic behaviour begin to wane soon after the relationship was established via marriage, co-owning property or having children with them and then continue to deteriorate over time to be replaced with you being increasingly subject to criticism and negative judgements?
- Do they vanish for long periods of time without apparent reason?
- Do you suspect their sexual history is far more promiscuous than what they have led you to believe?
- Do they (males) have stories about themselves and tales which seem heroic, amazing, dangerous and far-fetched, yet with no real proof of these adventures?
- Do they wake up in the mornings in a pool of sweat even in cold weather? Sometimes waking up next to them and the mattress is very damp, suspecting he/she may have urinated in their sleep?
- Do they have high testosterone levels? Upper body strength, high sex drive, impulsiveness or early baldness in males/pronounced Adam's Apple in females?
- Is there a sense of 'making love' being somewhat missing from the sex, as though everything they know about sex seems to be based on watching pornography?
- Do they (females) tell you they lost their virginity at an unusually young age and then claim that in their culture this is normal?
- Do they tolerate cold weather very well?

- Do they have unusual sweating, such as cold sweats after a short exercise?
- If they live alone, are their homes unkempt and if they have pets are the faeces not cleaned up regularly?
- Do they address themselves by a nickname, or by a title, as in, "Mr Jones thinks it's a good idea..." or "The Lieutenant says..." or "Stacy Shortcake thinks..."
- Is their handwriting an unintelligible scrawl, yet they sign their name with a sense of flair and importance?
- Are they unable to read or produce blueprints and plans?
- When they (female) were planning your wedding, did you feel like you were an afterthought — no more important than the flowers or music?
- Do they make incredibly ambitious plans and then change or abandon them halfway through or never actually start them at all?
- Do they repeat the same comments and anecdotes constantly — sometimes almost on queue?
- Do they (male) have a higher-than-normal interest in pornography and/or tend to prefer masturbation to lovemaking?
- Do they claim that the success of all the people in their lives, past and present only happened due to their doing them a favour and making them successful to begin with?
- Do they make annoying noises, whistles, humming or seem to mispronounce words deliberately to the point where you start to forget how they are supposed to be pronounced?
- When you are watching TV, have you ever noticed their eyes scanning the room — almost like a lizard looking for insects even though their head is facing the TV screen?
- When one of their parents died suddenly or was diagnosed with a terminal illness did they place an initial emphasis on possible wills, inheritances, or who was going to marry the surviving spouse in order to get

their money? Rather than demonstrate a real sense of loss or compassion for their surviving parent?

- Do they seem to have this notion that they are entitled to the best of everything without having to earn it?
- Do they never say 'thank you' nor show genuine appreciation for favours done with any real conviction?
- Does this individual interrupt you while you are speaking and complete your sentences with the outcome they determine and not what you were going to state?
- Does this person revel in being the centre of attention for no particular talent or ability?
- Do they act like they deserve medals and awards just for being who they are?
- Have you ever found yourself wondering if they are secretly bi-sexual (male) or even a different gender (female) in the past?
- Does this person ridicule and intensely criticise a product, store, restaurant, viewpoint, style, taste in music, travel and art which you enjoy, then only to witness them later on at some point aligning themselves with these same tastes and interests they mockingly condemned when you had expressed your enjoyment of them?

As soon as several of these red flags start to surface, and you are concerned you might be involved with a psychopath, I would suggest keeping a secret journal or logbook of any behaviour in the person which you find disturbing or unsettling. Make sure the person you are concerned about does not know this. If you alert them, they will simply use the information to alter their persona to manipulate you further by purposely playing down or eliminating the behaviours and mannerisms which you have pointed out. They are not being cured or rehabilitated when they adjust their idiosyncrasies. It is to refine their technique. They are not changing their ways. They are only altering/customising their bespoke persona which they use to work you more effectively.

ARE YOU A POTENTIAL TARGET?

- Are you recently widowed, divorced or in a difficult relationship?
- Are you financially responsible, solvent and secure? Such as a stable employment position/regular long term pay cheque with a government pension/full military pension?
- Were you abused, neglected, unloved by a parent/parents as a child?
- Did one or both of your parents die when you were a child or were you raised in a foster home or orphanage?
- Were you in the military as a young person?
- Are you very sensitive to emotional external stimuli, such as hearing certain music, or viewing a certain art work which can bring you to tears?
- Did you have a parent who was an alcoholic or a drug addict?
- Do you have a history of rescuing stray and injured animals?
- Do you have a strong desire to love and be loved?
- Are you living alone in a house on which the mortgage is fully paid off?
- Are you a recent educated immigrant with a degree or professional background and not yet fully aware of all the subtle cultural intricacies of your newly adopted country?
- Are you humbly unaware of your own special talents and abilities?
- Do you always give other people the benefit of the doubt at first?
- Did you lose a young child, are presently estranged from your children due to divorce or do you have a deep-rooted unfulfilled desire to raise and nurture a child of your own?
- Are you the kind of person who would get out of your car to help an old or handicapped person with their groceries?

- Do you think deeply about everyone and everything except yourself?
- Are you a single parent longing for a completed family?
- Do you have any special talent or ability which may bring you fame and wealth one day?
- Are you generally independent and self-supporting?
- Do you have a large disposable income?
- Do you believe that there is 'someone special' out there just for you and you let people know what kind of person this would be?
- Do you hide a sense of low self-esteem or hurt behind an outgoing and confident exterior due to a past emotional trauma you keep to yourself?
- Do you believe in 'love at first sight?'
- Do you feel incomplete without a 'soul mate'?

SEARCHING FOR THE FALSE PARADISE

There comes a point in all our lives where we have to begin a period of self-examination and inner reflection, taking stock of the kind of person we are and the image we project to others around us. Do we give off a caring, 'earth mother' energy? If so, why? Do you have a need to rescue people while fathering and mentoring those whom you perceive as needy and lost? What made you like this? Think back. You are an amalgamation of all the previous past experiences in your life which brought you to this point. Both the good and the bad experiences. They all count.

We need to become more selective in whom we wish to cherish, support and care for. It is not the personal duty of every individual to save the world as a whole, or the human race person by person. This message is given to us constantly by media and via other entities such as religion and nationalistic agendas. It serves the whole, but not the individual. Charity begins at home, compassion begins internally. We have to love ourselves first in order to attract the kind of people and situations to love us back in return. There is no way around this. We exist as individuals for a reason.

Unconditional love is conditional on loving oneself firstly and being secure in this. In the Garden of Eden we see this in the metaphor of Eve presenting Adam with the Fruit of Knowledge. Eve presents Adam with the apple not because she wanted to get him in trouble, but because she loved him enough to free his mind from the shackles of a spiteful and conditional God. Her handing the apple to Adam was her unconditional love for him and his humanity in totality and likewise, his acceptance of it was the same mutual respect and understanding returned back to Eve. However, it was highly significant that a woman implemented the process. Eve's only sin was to give birth to the intellect, and the intellect above all wants to be free.

Adam and Eve were made outcasts for thinking for themselves. This is why the Eden story and the concept of Original Sin is shoved in our faces by the psychopathic major religions. They want you to love the creed, the book, the pulpit and the dogma — they keep your eye *off* the ball. The psychopath in the relationship wants you to idolise him/her at the expense of yourself. The Serpent in the Garden of Eden represented Eve's 'self' in the psychological sense, transcending the superficial ego of eternity in superficial paradise for the full richness of life. Both good and bad.

Psychopaths are not a part of this aspect of humanity, but they are an important aspect of nature and are here for a reason. They are the grit which causes friction and pain and forces us to take care of ourselves and by extension the ones who really love and care for us in return. They are the ultimate expression of the overall evolutionary process. They are the 'Missing Link'. Without psychopathic dictators we would not have freedom fighters. Without psychopathic relationships we would not cherish the ones who really care for us. Compassion, empathy and kindness is as much a part of the evolutionary process as the DNA double helix. Mythology is as important as the microscope. Everything counts in order to construct your road map to a safe and secure future where no psychological predators will lie in wait ready to pounce around the next corner.

Taking care of oneself first and foremost is not being selfish, unpatriotic or uncaring. It is only when we discard the effect our own personal choices have upon others that it becomes a problem. This is how psychopaths function and operate; it is *their way or the highway* every time. We must and should look after ourselves while at the same time care for and cherish they who are truly deserving of our love. Sharing our love, affection, devotion and energy is a serious matter and should never be handed out freely to any person or entity who lobbies for this. If we overtly project the unconditional nurturer image to the rest of the world, then the predator will come calling.

The old cliché, *you are the one you have been waiting for* remains valid. Health and safety applies equally to our emotional, spiritual and psychological health as it does to our physical wellbeing. Look after yourself always. Be open and friendly, but not impulsive and easily swayed with superficial 'loving' gestures and displays from others. A small percentage of psychopaths are out there looking to parasite off your humanity. Be vigilant.

signs and symbols rule the world, not words nor laws.

Confucius

CHAPTER SIX
THE LEXICON OF THE RELATIVE AND THE ABSOLUTE

With its cosmology of subtle nuances and spellbinding enchantment, human behaviour remains as big a mystery to people as the complexities of the diesel combustion engine would be to a deer caught in the headlights of an oncoming truck. We are woefully and often willingly ignorant of the symbolic and intuitive world we inhabit. During the course of our daily contact with one another, the vast majority of our cognitive awareness and conceptual understanding of society and interactions with our fellow humans relies almost exclusively upon verbal and written communication.

The rest of the time we stare catatonically at television screens or print media where there is no dialogue, but a one-way monologue aimed at programming us. We are not engaged in any mutually beneficial conversation with televisions or newspapers — we are being *dictated to*. We have no control over the outcome of a TV show — the storyline, the unfolding plot or the conclusion. The 'cliff-hanger' at the end of each episode is there to keep us hooked, and we 'tune in next week at the same time, same channel' to be shown the outcome.

We spend the entire seven days in-between considering all the possible outcomes of the story. Then the carefully-placed shackles which the 'programmers' have harnessed to our collective psyches are dramatically unlocked as we sit down and listen to the opening credits of our favourite show as the title music begins.

You can actually feel your blood pressure change and your heartbeat alter in measured and meticulous stages of progression. Yet none of this is real — it is all make-believe.

During the commercial breaks we have our insecurities and personal expectations validated and serviced with a whole range of material, psychological and spiritual panaceas. We also didn't know that we wanted or even needed these remedies until the television advertisements told us so. Sit through an hour of primetime television and you'll discover exactly how the psychopathic predatory nature works on you, your community and your country. You are seduced into a false reality and the only thing the media-culture psychopathic delivery system in the guise of a TV has to accomplish to keep you interested is to make sure there is a cliff-hanger at the end so you keep coming back for more.

You will then begin to willingly love your servitude to the psychopathic storyline, characters and villains on TV because your reality has been altered to put you in this state of desire. The instinctual moral compass which you once had inside you has had its needle removed by mass-media and marketing and replaced with superficial targets you are told are to aspire to... *Buy this! Emulate her! Do this to be popular! Worship this hero!* and so on. All the psychopath has to do to gain absolute control over you is to constantly change the nature of this false reality you are mired in. The same thing happens in a marriage to a psychopath as it does with psychopaths ruling a nation and its media.

MIND CONTROL AND PREDATORY MEMORY.

Think you can't be mind-controlled? That you are far too educated, savvy and street-smart? That all your thoughts are your own, and that your personal opinions are carefully considered and formulated by your intellect? Are you really going to say you never voted for a politician because he or she made a promise or presented a manifesto which you believed they were sincere about? You have never bought a pointless consumer product on impulse? That you never worshiped in a building devoted to a dogma in which your only connection to this creed was that your parents brought you there as a child? That you never became emotionally involved in a movie scene where your eyes filled with tears even though the entire spectacle was filmed inside a studio set and the actors were just reciting lines someone else wrote for them? If you have managed to never have been subject to any of the above, then congratulations; you are the most intellectually and psychologically sovereign person who has ever lived. Or a psychopath.

The psychopath is akin to a star at the centre of their devious solar system of manipulated lives. The manipulated are akin to planets which ideally — from the psychopath's point of view — never escape the gravitational pull of the psychopath-star.

Psychopaths are the undisputed masters of mind-control. They do not do this by placing you under an intense light and filling you full of drugs, but by first evaluating you, then piecemeal and over time playing on and amplifying any gaps in your self-esteem. Before you know it, your thoughts and opinions are nearly all ones the psychopath has planted in your mind.

This is the main reason psychopaths are incredible copycats of their victims in the early days. *Tell me what you want and I'll become that* is the provisional mantra of the psychopath. The result: they have done such a thorough job of mirroring you and, in the early stages of seduction, stepping in to buoy you up in areas where they have sniffed out your weaknesses, you become completely psychologically dependent upon them for your entire sense of self and self-esteem.

In clinical studies of criminal psychopaths, Dr Robert Hare discovered that the hand gestures people make when speaking actually help our brains find words when we have difficulty expressing a complex concept, or if we are speaking a foreign language.

In a 1991 paper, Hare and his colleagues reported that psychopaths — particularly when talking about things they should find emotionally meaningful in terms of love for other people — produce a higher frequency of hand gestures than normal people, as though emotional concepts to a psychopath are akin to a foreign language.

By the same token, the psychopath is very aware when a potential victim is using hand gestures to explain a difficult concept and why. The psychopath will then 'aid' the victim by mirroring these gestures in order to convey the illusion that the psychopath can be subconsciously trusted. In time, this progresses to the psychopath interrupting the victim while they are speaking to a third party — before the victim can finish a sentence, the psychopath interrupts and finishes the sentence for them.

Eventually, the victim learns over time to either stop speaking altogether without the psychopath present or becomes a mimic of the psychopath's viewpoints. Either way, the mind of the victim has been subtly and perniciously reordered by the psychopath and the victim abdicates their natural ability for social interaction via one-on-one communication with others while the psychopath assumes the role of the victim's unofficial representative in public.

Psychopaths are always on the lookout for people they can successfully mind-control. In 2008, a study entitled *A Pawn by Any Other Name: Social Information Processing as a Function of Psychopathic Traits* was published by Dalhousie University, in conjunction with the University of British Columbia-Okanagan. The research team of Kevin Wilson, Sabrina Demetrioff and Stephen Porter invented a group of fictional characters from photographs of men and women with facial expressions conveying that they were either happy or unhappy. The researchers likewise created artificial biographical profiles indicating that some were financially successful while others were not. Included with each profile would be random information relating to various hobbies and interests of these fictional men and women. Before they took part in the study, the forty-four male undergraduate students were first given individual personality tests to establish their level of psychopathic behaviour.

Once the level of psychopathology had been determined, the students were then given the photos and biographical information about the fictional characters. Afterwards, the forty-four male undergraduate students were then asked to recall what they noticed or assumed about each of the fictional characters. The study concluded that participants with high levels of psychopathic traits demonstrated enhanced recognition for the unhappy, unsuccessful female character — the most vulnerable individual in the line-up of fictional characters. The authors of the study wrote, *"The high-psychopath participants demonstrated near-perfect recognition for this character."*

The researchers called this 'predatory memory.' The study also stated, *"Psychopathic traits, even in the absence of overt criminality, are associated with a cognitive style that is predatory in nature [and] in extreme cases, this may allow individuals with clinically diagnosable levels of psychopathy to spot vulnerable individuals for future exploitation."*

A vulnerable individual to a psychopath is like a blank canvas to an artist. The above study demonstrates how profoundly aware psychopaths are of a potential victim's emotional state and — by extension — their future potential for predatory mind-control after the psychopath is successful in implementing a relationship with the victim. The psychopath always makes a mind-controlled slave and prisoner of the other person(s) in a relationship.

It works equally well with a psychopathic employer and his staff, a psychopathic cult leader and his followers and most worrying of all, *the psychopathic elected leader and his subjects/citizens.* The psychopath will have already isolated you from your natural social network and support mechanisms before you realise you have been mind-controlled. Then the real show begins: to alter the very reality in which you exist. To make you question your own eyes, ears and other senses. To bombard you with agenda-driven lies. To blind you to the obvious and turn you into a zombiefied automaton while implementing a well-planned and brilliantly-executed distortion of your environment in order to destroy your interior psychological landscape.

GASLIGHTING

Gaslight is a classic Hollywood movie based on a play of the same name and the genesis of the term *gaslighting* as a way to describe how psychopaths alter reality around their victims, ultimately destroying their psychological sovereignty and eventually their sanity. This modus gives the psychopath complete control over the victim.

The original 1940's film is set in London in 1880 at the home of Jack Manningham and his wife. Bella Manningham is an emotionally drained woman who cannot make sense of her husband's clandestine disappearances from the house. He refuses to tell her where he is going while he is away, constantly deflecting the issue or playing down her concerns. Her anxiety is further compounded by his flirting with the female servants employed in their comfortable upper-middle-class home. Jack Manningham is intent on convincing his wife that she is going insane (this is where the inner psychopath takes over from the average cheating spouse) and in order to achieve this, he constantly turns down the level of the gas-powered lighting in their house.

When Bella brings the subject up, her husband tells her she is imagining all of it — that the lights are the same brightness they always have been. Eventually, a sympathetic policeman alerts Bella that she is married to a psychopath who is attempting to make her believe that she is going mad. The symbolism of the increasingly darkened rooms mirrors Bella Manningham's descent into the psychopathic labyrinth towards which her husband is pushing her. It is an extremely powerful and profound metaphor for the predatory mindset of the psychopath.

The term *gaslighting* has thus come to represent psychological mind control abuse in which false information is presented to the victim, altering their sense of reality and destroying the victim's faith in their own discernment.

Examples of gaslighting:

THE DEVIOUS CREEP AT WORK

A psychopathic employee at work lends you a music CD or piece of work-related equipment, and when you are done with it, you return it by placing it on their desk while the psychopath is not there. The psychopath later approaches you requesting its return. You tell them you left it on their desk, to which the psychopath claims they did not see it and can't find it either. You go with them to their desk to show them where you left it, and the psychopath — in full view of your fellow employees — tries to imply (often sarcastically) that you have stolen it, or they will instead 'find' the object broken, claiming that you damaged it. You cannot comprehend what you are hearing and begin to doubt your memory of what really happened is actually correct. You also feel you have lost the trust of the entire office as a result. Your work performance goes down as self-doubt and confusion — not to mention a sense of guilt or shame — enters your subconscious thoughts.

THE REVISIONIST PARENT

Your psychopath parent who may have abused and neglected you as a child may — years later when you are an adult and in front of others — glibly claim that you were 'spoiled' and were 'treated like a little prince or princess' when you were under their care. It will be stated in such a way that *you are somehow not grateful for this*, or *unaware of how lucky you were to have such a magnificent parent.* You have memories of none of this and can only recall being deprived proper care and parenting along with long periods of abuse and neglect.

Because they have heard the story repeated so many times growing up, younger members of the family may then begin to validate your psychopathic parent's version of your own personal history. You then begin to wonder if you imagined all the abuse and neglect. Having no witnesses other than the psychopathic parent further compounds your self-doubt while validating the psychopath's lies and fabrications. These psychopathically abusive parents may even go on to champion themselves publicly as defenders of children's rights and welfare as their own abused child or children looks on in disbelief.

THE 'RACE CARD' PLAYER

You are at a business meeting and having relaxing break-time banter with your colleagues, and you pass some innocent remark concerning the ethnic makeup of someone you all know. The psychopath will then remark something along the lines of, "I did not know you were a racist…"

Even when it was obvious to all around you that there was nothing derogatory, racist or offensive in your comments, the psychopath has planted an evil seed by accusing you of stereotyping someone racially. You fear that this may cost you your job, or at the very least your reputation among fellow staff—even though the other employees know you are not a racist. Will this story be reported to Human Resources? You can't believe the accusation made about you in front of your peers by this individual.

You are so taken aback by the psychopath's outrageous comment that it keeps you awake at night leading to a poor night's sleep and decreased on-the-job performance the next day. You also feel like your status and dignity has been compromised by the psychopath who accused you of being a racist. Worse still, you start to feel disturbed in the presence of the psychopath who made this remark as if your energy is being sapped by just being around them. You feel as if the psychopath is merrily keeping a dark secret about your personality from others which they can unleash to management at any time, destroying your reputation and your livelihood.

This nagging sensation constantly plays like a tape loop within your subconscious and affects you deeply. Your problem-solving abilities on the job deteriorate as you cannot concentrate, especially in the presence of the psychopath who made this remark, and your uneasiness and tension levels while in their presence simmer to a toxic boiling point. The psychopath knows this and is trying to get you to literally explode in rage so they have 'unstable' to add to 'racist' when they finally report you.

THE DEVIOUS DISCARDER

You are a man in a relationship with a female psychopath who needs the 'romance' to end quickly since they have found a new enabler who is getting serious and wants to fully legitimise that relationship. The psychopath now wants you out of the way with as little fuss as possible while making sure you do not do anything to jeopardise the new target's relationship with the psychopath. Very likely, the psychopath will now be pregnant, or have the new target out shopping for an engagement ring and is expecting a marriage proposal soon, so you'll have to be dumped in such a way that you do not get suspicious and discover what has really been going on.

It is also vital for the new target on the verge of a marriage proposal to not discover that he is being 'worked' too. He will also be assuming he is the 'special one' or the 'beloved'. It is also very likely there are several other males operating under a similar illusion that the female psychopath must dispose of in a hurry, however — in classic psychopath mode — in such a way that she can utilise them if need be in future. The sentiment, *'We can always be friends... '* being the potential conduit back to these men should they be needed again. The female psychopath will use phrases such as *'That golden rope between us will never break... '*

Upon being told by the female psychopath that she wants to end the relationship for some vague or cryptic reason, you stand your ground and demand answers regarding the sudden change, this lightning bolt out of the blue. When you continue to press for answers, the psychopath may then try a diversionary remark about you not being there for them when a family member died. You could have been on the other side of the world during this event and could do nothing about it, but suddenly the nature of the discussion has changed and it is no longer about why you are being dumped, but about you suddenly being put in the position of defending your own humanity.

The psychopath will then attempt to divert you into apologising to them, when the reality of the situation is that the psychopath is capitalising on the death of their own kin in order to make you feel you are at fault.

Ravaged with guilt, you can't comprehend that anyone would actually sink so low as to use the death of their family member as an excuse to shut you up. You have also been diverted from the real matter at hand — that the psychopath is disposing of you in a cold and casual manner in order to prey on someone new.

Even after the female psychopath has dumped you, they will often show their true colours by suddenly 'wanting you' once more, particularly if something happens in the interim to make you more of 'a catch'. The female psychopath will suddenly be back to the old persona they used to 'work you' and comments such as, *'You are the only one I ever really loved,'* are a classic technique — usually taking place while some other poor dummy is out shopping for an engagement ring.

THE 'CARING' PREDATOR

You are an elderly person under the care of a psychopath who entered your life as either a homecare agency worker, 'friend' or distant relative. They convince you that they could take better care of you if they moved into the spare room. At first it seems comforting and secure, fun even, but then things slowly start to unfold in a negative manner. Your routine has changed, then changes again, then changes constantly. You are at a loss as to why this confusion is suddenly the order of the day. You go to bed when it is daylight, being told it is late. Furniture is changed and moved around in the rooms while you were asleep. Photos have been replaced in frames which once contained images of your family. You are watching a TV programme and the carer comes in and switches the channel. When you remark you were watching a particular show, the psychopath claims that the channel hasn't been changed and you are still watching the same TV show.

You begin to wonder why your friends no longer call on you and other care providers such as cleaners no longer come to the house. Strangers of the opposite sex to the psychopathic carer are coming and going to and from your house and you are not sure who they are or why they are staying overnight. The psychopath tells you they are going out for the evening and you hear the front door being shut, but later you hear banging and moving noises in the basement or in the attic and are terrified you are all alone in the house with an intruder. As an isolated elderly person you can't wait for the psychopath carer to 'return' and save you. Upon returning, the psychopath might make a comment that they believe you completely, since they think the house is 'haunted'. The carer then tells you that you would be better off in a retirement home. In order to pay for this you must sign over your home and savings to the psychopath who will arrange everything for you.

THE 'PROTECTIVE' OVERLORDS

You have been made to believe by media and politicians that a certain ethnic or religious tradition is behind all the terrorist activities, and this has to result in increased security for all.

One day, you are waiting with your family to get on a flight and you have to walk through a full-body scanner which reveals your nakedness to the security staff, along with that of your wife and nine year-old daughter. Then you noticed that two women dressed in the traditional religious wear of the so-called terrorist background are allowed to bypass the naked scanner on account of religious sensitivities. You can't understand what is going on. The politicians are treating you and your family like terrorists — yet the ones who they tell you are most likely to be terrorists are excluded from these demeaning and invasive security requirements.

Your psychology has been so shattered, filled with fear, confused and bewildered that eventually you succumb to all kinds of social and personal restrictions, ultimately believing that you and your family are the real potential terrorists and need to be protected from yourselves. The innocent members of the so-called 'terrorist' profile group are further subjected to media and political stigma and bigotry by the same politicians and pundits who defend their right to not pass through the naked body scanner. It makes no sense on any level because it's not meant to — it is *gaslighting* inflicted on all of society by a psychopathic government and media.

Psychopaths will not flinch from gaslighting their victims in order to get what they want — your absolute psychological, sexual, emotional and financial submission to the psychopath. Upon gaining this domination, the psychopath will eventually discard you and walk away as if you never existed. You'll be left a shattered husk of your former self, wondering who you are now and what happened to the person you once were. But there is hope. The one thing they can never take from you is your spirit. That's not for negotiation — even if the psychopath made you think so at the time.

PSYCHOPATHS AND BULLYING

One of the most common misconceptions relating to the pathology is that deep down, psychopaths are filled with self-loathing and they project their inner hatred of themselves onto their victims. Nothing could be further from the truth. To imply this is to suggest that psychopaths are somehow self-reflective. What is being classified as self-loathing is in reality more akin to resentment and jealousy. They do not feel inferior to other people who enjoy relationships, social life, careers and material goods — they just want to take these things away from the victims for the sake of a sick game of one-upmanship, destroying another person's life for a brief rush of energy.

This resentment is most commonly seen when psychopaths bully other adults. They start this in school and they continue to do this for the rest of their lives. Bullying pays off for the psychopath on many levels towards their social and employment ambitions.

Although a psychopath will implement a smear campaign against another person at work or in an organisation in order to take over that person's position, the underlying thrust is that it is the position the victim holds that the psychopath finds desirable. If it le ads to the bullied victim resigning, transferring to another department or even killing themselves (murder-by-suicide) then so be it.

Neuroscientists have established that the human brain continues to grow and change long after the rapid developmental stage of early childhood. It is now well-established that people who have been bullied as children by a psychopathic parent or student at school, or as an adult at work — are much more likely to be depressed, anxious, and suicidal.

The psychological torment that victims of bullying experience is emotionally ravaging and visceral. Bullying has now been shown to leave a lasting effect on a young person at a time when their brain is still developing, actually leading to reduced electrical connectivity within the brain, as well as destroying the growth of new neurons.

This very real neurological damage is identical to what is seen in those who have been physically and sexually abused in childhood.

A paper by the neuroscientist Martin Teicher in the July 2010 edition of the *American Journal of Psychiatry* outlined a study of the effects on children being verbally abused by adults and their peers and presented some unsurprising data giving scientific legitimacy to what victims of bullies have long known.

In his study of more than 1,000 young people, he discovered that words were indeed as hurtful as 'sticks and stones'. Teicher's participants varied in how much taunting, ridicule, criticism, shouting, and bad language they had been subject to in the past, but what was revealed was that victims of bullying had higher incidences of depression, anxiety, and other psychiatric disorders than the subjects who had not experienced bullying.

Those subjects who reported having been bullied by their peers had observable abnormalities in a part of the brain known as the corpus callosum, connecting the right and left hemispheres of the brain, vital for visual processing, and (very significantly, from a psychopathic standpoint) *clarity of memory*.

Victims of psychopathic relationships always have trouble recalling memories from the time their relationship with the psychopath commenced. Psychopaths will often say to their victims. *'Do you recall when you said this... ?'* and so forth, and the victim will often reply that they have no memory of doing and saying certain things which the psychopath claimed they did indeed do and say. The victims' memories are impaired. This allows the psychopath to invent a fake past event which the victim cannot readily dispute. This is why it is very common for psychopaths to target people who were victims of childhood abuse and bullying.

In another study, Tracy Vaillancourt, a psychologist at the University of Ottawa, discovered that being bullied as a child can alter levels of cortisol, a hormone produced during times of stress. Vaillancourt's findings showed that boys who have been bullied have higher levels of cortisol than normal, while bullied girls have abnormally low levels. This weakens the victim's immune system, sometimes destroying neurons and again leading to memory problems.

More and more studies are finding verbal bullying is more akin to physical and sexual abuse than had been previously assumed. As psychopaths perform all three on their victims it becomes very apparent how a skilled psychopath can break down and destroy even the most rational and emotionally-balanced person. If the target has been bullied as a child, this creates a perfect opportunity for the psychopath to implement techniques such gaslighting to greater effect and much sooner into the relationship. The psychopathic child who is bullying other children at school, or the psychopathic parent bullying his/her own children can be viewed in the same context as a farmer planting an apple orchard to be harvested later on in life.

The Silent Treatment

Another aspect of bullying which the psychopath uses to deflect their shortcomings onto their victim is *the silent treatment*. It is very common among psychopaths who specialise in taking control of small social groups as a kind of ringleader of pathetic individuals which the psychopath then manipulates by playing on their vast array of insecurities and low intelligence. The psychopath will then cultivate these individuals into proto-psychopaths in order to socially banish the targeted individual.

This sadistic agenda was very popular with British and Irish trade unions in the 1960's and 70's when the term 'being sent to Coventry' became a kind of code word to socially isolate individuals within a factory or other industrial working environment. The ultimate aim would be to get the isolated individual to commit suicide, which tragically did indeed happen in countless cases. In many instances, this inhuman tactic was fully endorsed and actively encouraged by trade union leadership in order to copper-fasten union members into an 'us and them' mentality.

Similar to using projection — in this case, the silent treatment — the victim very often has no idea what they have done to offend the psychopath. The silent treatment is often undertaken with the psychopath's 'useful idiots' and collaborators who have been encouraged to join in. In a school, office or organisational scenario, this can spring from the psychopath holding some deep resentment or jealousy towards the targeted individual and could be based on little more than the victim being more emotionally positive, attractive, socially liked, higher paid or even in a happy relationship.

A psychopath can keep the silent treatment going for years until the victim succumbs and accepts responsibility for any blame from the psychopath. Barring the victim committing suicide or leaving for good, the psychopath will ensure the victim begs them to come for 'peace' talks where the victim will unquestioningly acquiesce to all the psychopath bully's demands. This can be a risky game for many psychopathic bullies to play if they implement the silent treatment on a strong-willed or well-liked individual, in case it blows up in the psychopath's face, leaving them socially isolated instead.

If the silent treatment does eventually backfire, the psychopath will 'break the ice' — often completely out of the blue — with some glib statement about how *'this is rather silly, you know!'* even though the person on the receiving end of the silent treatment neither implemented nor wanted the silent treatment to happen in the first place. The psychopath's plan derails and it is ultimately the psychopath who has to surrender.

Often, psychopaths can be social risk takers who, through impulsiveness in implementing bullying or the silent treatment, fail to grasp the long-term outcome should the target refuse to give in. Usually this ends up with on-lookers being either amused or repulsed by the absurdity of the psychopath as they realise the emperor indeed has no clothes.

Likewise, the psychopathic bullying parent implementing the silent treatment on a child may find they have no children or grandchildren to enable them in their later years. Not that they learn from the experience. They will simply utter phrases such as, *My own child abandoned me!* or *I was a team player and they all stabbed me in the back…*

we have no right to ask
why sorrow comes unless
we also ask the same
question for every
moment of happiness.

CHAPTER SEVEN
SANCTUARY

Before we begin to regain our personal sovereignty we must first safeguard that our contact with the psychopath is permanently cut and disconnected. This is a crucial step, as in the case of a romantic relationship you may find yourself missing the psychopath to a far greater degree than you ever experienced compared to a normal relationship break-up. The tender moments and loving memories you have of the psychopath are not real in any meaningful way. They are devoid of any substance. You are longing for a phantom, an actor in a play, a chimera , not a loving individual who cared about you beyond your usefulness to them.

Even so, you have to maintain the state of permanent disconnect no matter how much in the early days you are longing to talk to them once more. Chances are, you feel this way based on the falsehood you also have assumed about yourself, coupled with the psychopath's custom persona invented to manipulate you. You may still be in love, however, *you were in love with a persona invented to work you* — the psychopath's perfectly-constructed piece of theatre tailor-made for your psychological needs. It was never love. It was an illusion. The romance wasn't real. There was no love story. You are also addicted to the effects of a persona invested with the high levels of testosterone all psychopaths have, and is particularly strong with female psychopaths. It becomes a sexual drug. Now you must go cold turkey.

Psychopaths are indeed appalling individuals who cause colossal social and personal misery. The aftermath of having being caught within their control grid by personal manipulation is profoundly traumatic for victims and society at large. From our journey through this long, dark tunnel and upon our emergence into the light, I believe that we evolve into more complete people. Because of the experience we have endured in the clutches of control and manipulation we have learned something the psychopath can never know and we grow, while they just have a momentary spasm of success before their inevitable downward trajectory begins once again.

In the long run, we will always be the real winners , but first we have to disconnect from the psychopathic control grid forever. This is where the victim's personal responsibility to themselves takes precedent. If you ever want a life you can call your own, then you have no choice.

If you have spent any time allowing the psychopath to do your thinking for you, you will find that the main reason you may 'miss them' is that *you need them to tell you straight out why they left you.*

Realise that *needing the psychopath for anything at this point is time and energy wasted — they were never interested in giving you what you needed in the first place.* Instead, it was the complete opposite — you only ever existed to serve *their needs.* Your 'thinking for yourself muscle' is simply out of shape from lack of use. Now's the time to get it working again by admitting that the only 'closure' you will ever have is what you give yourself.

The psychopath — be it the crazy boss or the 'lover' who casually dumped you — will often try to keep an open line of communication with you. Not because they miss you, but because you may be useful to them in future. DISCONNECT from the psychopath absolutely and completely. *No Contact Ever Again* (NCEA), no communication, and above all, do not fall for the *'we can still be friends'* routine. All that means to the psychopath is, *'I am using a handsaw right now, but you are the best hammer I ever had, so stay on the shelf where I can get to you if I need you for something the handsaw cannot do.'*

Remaining friends is seen as a form of open-ended negotiation by the psychopath to win you back if needed, or manipulate you again in future. Or they may just want to amuse themselves with you now and again to deal with their boredom. This could be something as twisted as enjoying watching you suffer emotionally as they tell you about their new relationship and life without you.

They are demented and twisted beyond the comprehension of normal human beings. They have no more love for their new partner(s) than they had for you and this is what makes your heartbreak so pointless — the psychopath's new enabler is just as much a stepping stone as you were. The psychopath may even try to bargain some common understanding, a common ground of 'mutual understanding' the two of you can come to agree on. *Do not negotiate.*

There is no such thing as complete closure to a psychopath. They all maintain a list of past, present and potential victims in a kind of league table rating of possible future utility. You haven't so much been completely discarded by the psychopath — it is more a case of being relegated further down the list while someone else is moved up to the top of the league. You are currently on the lower ranks among previous 'useful idiots' and enablers. Your time will more than likely come again as the psychopath browses through their little black book of past victims.

Expect the psychopath to return to your doorstep someday to profess their eternal devotion to you, professing how they made a terrible mistake hurting you. How you are the only person who can save them.

Translation: *'Alright, so I have ruined your life. Destroyed the person you once were. Ruined your finances and faith in the human race as a whole. But you have to realise that it is actually your fault and I am the real victim here. But I forgive you.'*

Sometimes, the psychopath will resort to hysterical behaviour. Hysteria and psychopathy was confirmed as long ago as 1967 by the American Journal of Psychiatry in the paper *Hysteria and Antisocial Behavior: Further Evidence of an Association.* Ignore the high drama and the 'on bended knee' tear-filled pleadings — it's nothing more than an indicator of the relative intensity of psychopath's current need for a place to live, or a loan, or simply a warm body for the night.

You may find that permanently disconnecting from the psychopath will be difficult. Depending upon your resolve, this may take anything from months to years. In the case of a psychopathic workplace environment there are very real and immediate financial implications. You may be ravaged by resentment and bitterness. You must not allow the psychopath, or anyone else the psychopath could be using as a 'middle man,' to lure you back by playing on your financial or psychological state in the immediate aftermath. You are being tested by the psychopath so they can evaluate how much they have broken you. No Contact Ever Again. While shunning them infuriates the psychopath, your task will be to let go of the desire to witness their discomfort because *they will never show it to you*. But hear this:

Nothing infuriates them more than the one who got away for good.

Going back to the psychopath even as 'a friend' will only prove to the psychopath once and for all that you are a willing slave.

Keep your dignity. You'll be heartbroken, insecure, maybe even impoverished for a while, but consider this the labour pains of your rebirth. What is on the other side will be more fulfilling and rewarding than what you left behind. If you return to the psychopath control grid your reward will be your death — of your dignity, of your psyche, of your personality, of your self-esteem. In short, the death of your soul. The slow, painful and pointless self-sacrifice of all your beautiful human potential. You did not manifest into the world in order to be looked upon and treated as an object, a device or a means to someone's else ends.

As Patrick McGoohan announces in the role of the unbreakable Number 6 during the opening titles of the profoundly deep and insightful 60s classic *The Prisoner*,

> *"I will not make any deals with you. I've resigned. I will not be pushed, filed, stamped, indexed, briefed, debriefed or numbered. My life is my own. I resign."*

Let statements like this become your mantra. Makes no difference if the psychopath was your former spouse/partner, your ex-boss, or control freaks in government buildings where the biggest psychopaths of all can be found *en masse*. You are not someone else's plaything for their amusement, personal gain or gratification. When you disconnect absolutely from the manipulation and the deceit, you are saying to the psychopath in the clearest possible manner,

"I am a sovereign, independent person and you are not in control of me or my life and never will you be allowed to exploit, manipulate or use me again — you are dead to me."

Then walk away forever.

If you have to maintain contact with the psychopath due to joint custody of children, wrapping up a business you co-owned with them, or having to remain at your job to keep a roof over your children's heads and food on their table and you have exhausted all other options with no other recourse, then minimal contact *with witnesses* when in the presence of the psychopath must apply. You must implement a plan of action to deal with all and every possible tactic the psychopath will use on you.

EXIT STRATEGIES

When you are still at a job and have to deal with the psychopath, let any friends at work know about psychopaths in the workplace and how they operate. But do not do it from a place of fear and paranoia. Be casual and remain positive while relaying this information about the psychopath to your trusted co-workers.

Do not approach any of the psychopath's useful idiots or clueless enablers with this information. Once this seed is planted in a person's subconscious it grows very slowly — but it still grows. It is an interesting process and can be incredibly empowering to engineer and implement. Along with NCEA, it is one of the few actions a victim can undertake in order to give a psychopath something to really annoy them.

Although many people are oblivious to the fact that they live in a world where psychopaths are all around them, and in all walks of life, they have most certainly experienced the pathological after-effects of psychopathology enough to want to take an interest in the subject and learn more about it. It may be enough to have the psychopath realise that the current hunting ground is not as fertile with gullible morons as they thought and they may move to another job.

Another vital measure if you must deal with a psychopath is to always have a witness when talking to them. For example, if the psychopath gets you in a corner and says, *"We should do this and that with this account/project"* and you reply, as clearly as you can without shouting, *"So you are saying, John, that we should… ?"*

Often you will notice the psychopath looking around to see if anyone else has heard you. Another time, come back to him or her at their desk when others are around and again in a loud but calm, casual voice say things like, *"You know John… when you were saying that we should do this with the project…"* State this in such a way others hear it clearly. Chances are the psychopath will have fed a different story about the same situation/scenario to someone else within hearing range. This will be the nearest the psychopath will ever get to showing panic.

Now, here is the most important part: *Do not show fear, confusion or any sign the psychopath is rattling you emotionally.* By this I mean that even if the psychopath is driving you mad, say nothing and make an excuse about getting more coffee or using the bathroom and leave the area. Also, keep your mouth shut around the psychopath about EVERYTHING other than the matter at hand. They will use any personal information you give them against you later. Tell them nothing about your life, your relationships or anything other than business talk.

Uncovering their Messy Past

Finally, this is well worth doing: if you can afford it and if it is legal in your country, get a background check done on the psychopath. Chances are you could uncover a bombshell. They could be using a false identity or never went to the college they claim to have attended, and if you get some damning past information on them, put it in an envelope and mail it to everyone in the company including the senior managers. Include yourself on the list of addresses so you will be as 'shocked' as everyone else. The same applies to inter-office typed memos. Make sure they do not know it is you who did this. That's why acting and remaining cool, calm and emotionally neutral around the psychopath is important at all times.

Often, just knowing and accepting in your heart that you are aware of psychopaths and have good knowledge of them and their behaviour is usually enough to drive them away. Since they are fundamentally lazy, they simply move on to an easier target. Buy books such as *The Sociopath Next Door* and *Snakes in Suits*, carry them into the office and leave them face up on your desk with the titles clearly visible for the psychopath. You would be amazed how nearly psychic psychopaths can seem at times, and they most assur-edly do not like it when they realise you might be on to them. Your awareness of psychopaths and psychopathology can spread like a virus to others around you, though this can only happen if you de-fend yourself from a place of calm and dignified resolve, devoid of fear or obvious hatred.

If you are an employer concerned about workplace psychopaths, organise a seminar or have speakers on the subject come to the office for a workshop. This can be very useful for rooting out the psychopaths among your staff. Take notice of which ones were not present at these seminars, or tried to belittle and mock the idea when it was first suggested.

Unavoidable Contact with Psychopathic Ex

If you are divorced or separated from a psychopath and have chil-dren with them, the psychopath will use the children as pawns to control you. A friend of mine found himself in this situation — he discovered having a witness around as much as possible, even bringing a friend along, forced the psychopath to behave. He car-ried a video camera and kept it on all the time and told her he was running a camera and would point it at her if she went into full drama mode, or started cursing around the child. He said this 'rat-tled the hell out of her' and she had no idea how to handle it. He also told me that not making eye-contact with his psychopathic ex-wife while around her was very empowering as her stare would unnerve him.

In the end he got full custody of his son since she didn't want the child for anything other than a pawn (usual story) and he was lucky enough to be done with her completely. So if you have a child with a psychopath, try getting full custody. Psychopaths — regardless of playing Super Parent for the masses — generally find their children a pain and a drain on their time and attention since they really don't want them for anything except power and control over the other parent or to take care of the psychopath in their old age. Let your lawyer handle all negotiations while going through a divorce or custody process with a psychopathic ex. Make sure to educate your legal representative on the true nature of psychopaths and how they function.

Mobile phone video cameras are a superb tool when engaging with psychopaths and con artists in general. During the next election, when some politician comes to your door looking for your vote, let them know you are filming them and then see how many promises they make. You will find that terms previously used by the politician such as *I will* and *absolutely* and *I fully promise* will be replaced with *we'll see*, or *maybe* or *I can't guarantee…*

If the politician protests that you are filming them on your doorstep, just remind them that political representatives seem to have no problem filling our streets with CCTV cameras pointed at us and that you are just returning the compliment. I can assure you the look on their faces will be priceless. Better still, make a suggestion that when they get elected they should install CCTV in every office in government buildings with a camera pointing at the desk of every elected representative and senior public servant with twenty-four hour Internet access, 'in the interest of preserving democracy and public safety,' of course.

The top rules of unavoidable engagement with the psychopath in all situations are to…

- Keep your mouth shut as much as possible
- Set the agenda on your terms and
- If you feel yourself getting upset just walk away and show no anger or frustration in front of them.

Never be alone with these predators and if you are, record everything they say and do and let them know at the time that you are doing this.

THE DANGERS OF RUMINATION

The damage which a psychopath may have inflicted on an individual can linger for many years afterwards in the form of depression and negative thinking. The psychopath is very aware of this. They revel in this constant drip-feed of emotional turmoil and grief they leave within others.

Most victims of psychopaths socially isolate themselves, often for years at a time, dwelling on the negatives and finding themselves spiralling deeper and deeper into depression. Psychologists refer to this as rumination — repeating negative thoughts, dwelling continually upon regret, recalling conversations and mentally replaying all the things they wish they had said yet doing nothing to change the situation.

Victims end up over-thinking, trying to make sense, trying to get *the answer*. Often, this leads to distorted rationalisations such as declaring anyone and everyone who has ever annoyed, offended, hurt or damaged them in some manner to be a sociopath, narcissist, psychopath, and so on. This is tragic on two counts as it leads to the social destruction of the ruminating individual, while also allowing real psychopaths off the hook by allowing them to say, *"Oh they claim everyone who ever pissed them off to be a psychopath!"* Rumination is a very toxic trap which victims must strive to remove themselves from as soon as possible before it becomes their de-facto lifestyle.

THE DEEPER DETOX

More than anything else, look after yourself. Try not to drink too much or eat bad food that causes indigestion at night such as Mexican, curries and cheese-filled foods. Natural remedies like valerian can help you have a great sleep without side effects. Sleep is very important since psychopaths use their victim's sleeplessness to further blur their reactions the next day. Spend the weekend in the countryside if you can and do not watch TV shows or movies, or listen to songs which have underlying psychopathic themes, which is most movies, songs and television shows these days.

Better still, get rid of your TV completely and try to develop a more creative and natural way of living. You'll soon discover beautiful people and situations will flow back into your life in the wake of the psychopath's departure.

New financial opportunities and projects will also suddenly appear too. It is almost as though the psychopath in your life was an energy blockage, a kind of devious dam preventing the flow of all good things to and from you. Everything is energy and the universe wants to make you happy if you remove the psychopath standing between you and your true path in this life.

The Sanskrit term *dharma* refers to your natural or proper state. Cultivate it by discovering who your true friends are, the ones who really cared and loved you all along. The most beautiful gift of all is discovering yourself after breaking the chains of psychopathic bondage.

And what happens to the psychopath? Who cares?

never, never brave me, nor my fury tempt: downy wings but wroth they beat; tempest even in reason's seat.

Herman Melville

CHAPTER EIGHT

THE EQUAL OPPORTUNITY PREDATOR

In an age where diversity is quite rightly cherished and universally promoted as a symbol of tolerance and enlightenment, the enterprising psychopath can at least claim to be well ahead of the game. There is no group more diverse in society than psychopaths. They are everywhere, in every race, religion, sexual orientation, social class, profession and political party. Psychopaths have done sterling work deeply entrenching themselves within all and every aspect of humanity. From the gilded halls of palatial mansions to the corrugated-roof shanty towns and all points in between, they prey amongst us. Soulless, pernicious automatons obsessed exclusively with ownership, control and survival. Psychopaths all seem to abide by some unwritten 'predators agreement' whereby they unofficially avoid each other's hunting ground. Plenty of prey for all.

One of the reasons circus clowns terrify sensitive individuals is because their image triggers an instinctual response within us concerning a collective archetypal folk memory of the potential evil which might lay behind the painted-on smile. We know the smile of the circus clown is fake and that underneath the expression can be a malicious sneer.

When one considers how vast the average psychopath's sphere of influence can be, it is not surprising that they sometimes go the extra mile in order to find enablers and 'useful idiots'. They can travel as far a becoming a civil rights activist in order to move (prey) among other races outside the psychopath's own ethnic group.

They can even go as far as becoming a transsexual in order to win female-only sports tournaments if they were not good enough to make it as a male athlete. If anyone questions their devious motives and their 'cheating at any cost' solution, they can simply claim that others are being 'bigoted and narrow-minded'.

Psychopaths are always, and I mean always, the first ones to shout, *Racist!* or *Homophobe!* or *Whacko conspiracy theorist!* at anyone who may be on to them and their agenda. Especially if the other person is coming from a standpoint which undermines the current belief package which the psychopath has bought into — usually as part of an invented persona they need to validate. Psychopaths feel deeply unsettled by anyone who can think for themselves and not accept blindly any information which is fed to them by authority figures, media and social peer pressure. This is why so many of them either officially or unofficially assume the role of social watchdogs — Orwellian 'thought police,' if you will. Psychopaths are not only unable to 'think outside the box' but they have an unconscious, instinctual drive to make sure nobody else does either.

Psychopath-spotting on Internet message boards can be a highly interesting hobby in its own right. Generally, when someone comes on to a discussion group or is even a long-term member of a group and they specialise in a subject unknown to the moderators, or when they represent a viewpoint outside the accepted psychological/cultural paradigm set by the moderators, they will be instantly declared 'trolls' or 'disruptive posters' and banned from the group. Psychopaths who are not moderators will shoot down the poster — mocking and ridiculing them without actually debating the point being made, because *they can't debate effectively and do not want to be exposed for this lack.*

All psychopaths, when you take away their deviousness, are usually morons and imbeciles. They are forever in survival mode, defending their patch against anything which endangers their hunting — this includes their common tactic of shutting down open dialogue which may undermine the psychopath's authority, either through censorship or ridicule. The biggest perceived danger being that the empathic, intelligent folks may start whispering in the woodshed.

I was told a story of a psychopath from a small rural town in New Zealand who from an early age took notes of the comings and goings of the local inhabitants, compiling what was essentially dossiers on them. Later, as a student frequenting Internet message boards, they would record and log IP addresses and other computer details of posters who opposed them and then use this to 'win' arguments or simply ridicule them by digging up old forum posts which had nothing to do with the debate at hand. By the same token, the psychopath set his own messages *to not be archived by the server* so nobody could do the same to him in return. That's psychopathic ethics and control for you.

I was told later that this individual became a political journalist reprinting government and corporate press releases as if they were undisputed facts, though completely devoid of any political or commercially-orientated bias.

Such deeply distorted psychopathic individuals also make ideal recruits for organisations as the CIA, NKVD, MI5/MI6, KGB, Mossad, and Stasi where their psychopathic need for pathological voyeurism, planting false evidence, destroying lives and gaining a rush from power trips is fully covered by criminal immunity from their actions. Indeed, even psychopaths who are not employed with national security organisations very commonly make up stories that they are *secret agents working undercover*. Of course, some of them actually do find employment in secret service agencies worldwide where they are paid to be psychopaths in all but title.

In late 2010, an eight-month investigation entitled Project Flicker revealed that 5200 employees of the CIA and other US Government security agencies purchased child pornography and were neither prosecuted or even investigated. Hardly conjures up images of suave James Bond types at the roulette table with a supermodel on either side, now does it?

High-ranking public servants getting little more than a slap on the wrist (if even that) for indulging in activities which would land you or me in prison seems to be a common occurrence everywhere.

Some politically-connected psychopaths do get punishment now and again, particularly if they are low ranking nobodies who go a bit further than just being paedophiles. Politically Correct mass murderer Dennis Nielsen, who strangled and dismembered sixteen gay men in the 1980s, was a highly-active member of Labour Party fringe groups such as the Anti-Nazi League. When he wasn't busy boiling people's heads in a pot or masturbating over the corpses of his victims, he reportedly was a self-righteous, sanctimonious armchair socialist declaring anyone a 'racist' or 'homophobe' for not living up to his own high standards of social and ethical responsibility. When Nielsen was told by the police that human remains were found in the drains of his London apartment, he exclaimed, *"Good grief, how awful!"*

Even though Dennis Nielsen was a very rare example of a physically violent psychopath, the well-established psychopathic fake morality and superficial empathy for marginalised groups in order to make them appear compassionate and ethically-superior is clearly apparent.

It makes no difference if their pathology extends no further than leeching off another person's hard work. The psychopath will not refrain from issuing self-glorifying platitudes about their work ethic and 'doing a fair day's work for a fair day's pay,' because they do not get that words have underlying meanings and are not just scripted phonetic mutterings to be issued forth at opportune moments.

What is even more depressing is how the corporate media handwringing 'journalists' and editors from the same newspapers which play down government-official psychopath stories frequently then hand themselves awards for freedom of speech and protecting the public interest. Most people are aghast and outraged when they finally see this hypocritical selective censorship for what it is. It's hardly surprising more and more people look for independent journalism on blogs and other news sources, which is why mainstream newspapers and news agencies are becoming increasingly dependent on government assistance to remain in business. Propaganda doesn't come cheap nowadays.

The alternative and usually far more accurate and credible news sources are naturally enough being declared 'unreliable' by corporate and government propagandists in all the mainstream media outlets, which — interestingly enough — our bizarre New Zealand psychopath mentioned earlier is gleefully employed in.

With its sanctimonious pathological culture of 'editorial slants' and 'generally accepted truths,' mainstream political journalism also prides itself on shooting down marginal opinions in the interest of 'free speech and freedom of expression.' This is not to say all mainstream journalists are instinctual Ministry of Information-style psychopaths. Many are, but many others are unknowingly operating under the psychopathic control grid. Honest journalists, like honest politicians, generally do not make it beyond the local scene.

BEING CYNICAL TOWARDS AUTHORITY FIGURES IS HEALTHY AND NATURAL

We must not be afraid to question or challenge authority. We must not be bullied into accepting the *status quo* by anyone, especially strangers or faceless authority figures. This is healthy — this builds self-esteem and confidence. Having a healthy cynical approach to the information which we are presented with makes us less likely to be targeted and manipulated by psychopaths. Yale University psychologist Stanley Milgram, in his remarkable and frankly disturbing 1974 book entitled, *Obedience to Authority: An Experimental View*, detailed an experiment whereby participants in a controlled study were ordered to increase the intensity of what they believed to be electric shocks to a subject in another room, demonstrating just how dangerous blind obedience to authority can be.

After the subjects were informed that they would be absolved of any personal legal consequences, sixty-five percent of the participants technically murdered the person on the receiving end of the electric shocks. All it took was an authority figure to instruct them to increase the voltage until the person on the other side of the wall was 'dead' from 450 volts of current. Even though the person screaming for mercy was an actor who received no actual electric shocks, more than half the participants who believed it was a real test 'killed' him in order to show their obedience to the authority figure. Unfortunately, the experiment did not evaluate the subjects for their level of psychopathic tendencies prior to the tests, though I expect it would have yielded some useful data.

QUESTION EVERYTHING

A person in any kind of a relationship with a psychopath is always expected to align their world view with that of the psychopath. Free-thinking on behalf of the non-disordered associate, friend, partner, spouse or other family member results in 'the silent treatment' and/or ridicule. This will persist until the victim ends up buying into the same belief package as the psychopath. Threats of abandonment or even humiliation in front of others will be used to bring about the acquiescence crucial to the psychopath. A personal intellectual — or especially spiritual — journey undertaken by the spouse or partner of the psychopath will not be tolerated to any degree that might undermine the psychopath's domestic control.

Thoughtcrime is the psychopath's most beloved tactic in order to control information and ideas or to distract from cold hard facts — both at a personal level and at a social level different from the agenda of the psychopath. They will go to incomprehensible lengths to deny any wrongdoing or mistake on their behalf or on behalf of anything they have connected themselves to.

They will look to control all the flow of information, spending hours online looking up other people's posts and comments left on websites. If a psychopath can develop the skills to become proficient at computers they will sometimes turn to hacking to gain access to personal files and private information on colleagues, family, friends or neighbours. This is why so many of them are recruited as secret police and informers by totalitarian regimes.

As mentioned previously, claiming to be part of an oppressed minority or group or defending a 'morally' popular opinion is utilised constantly by psychopaths to deflect criticism of themselves and their actions. Female psychopaths in particular are very quick to use the sexism card or claim sexual harassment when confronted. Failing that, female psychopaths always have Borderline Personality Disorder as their ace in the deck to show how you are picking on an 'unwell woman who needs understanding and support!' Even when you find her in bed with your best friend having sex on a pile of money she just withdrew from your bank account while you were out working to earn it.

BORDERLINE PERSONALITY DISORDER

Mainstream science has brought many wonderful and vital discoveries to humanity. However, regardless of whether or not they like to admit it, the mental health field of research has been riddled with crackpot and agenda-driven theories which become 'fact' as soon as enough money is thrown at it. Corporate and governmental necessities have paid off some scientists to come to certain 'consensuses' regardless of data and research.

Crackpot scientific fads include Racial Hygiene/Eugenics, the most rabidly-defended field of its day by top scientists and universities worldwide, shortly before a particular short Austrian started designing black uniforms.

The late 20th century obesity epidemic in the West augmented by the scientific endorsement of the Low Fat/High Carbohydrate diet, the bizarre addition of the deadly poison Sodium Fluoride to municipal drinking waters as a 'topical' dental treatment, the media-driven eyeball-bugging hysteria surrounding the 2009 Swine Flu 'epidemic', all have shown that science has now and again — certainly more than they care to admit — been shown to be almost comically flexible in its beliefs, depending upon the corporate/government grant money being waved in front of the researchers.

There is also a small, but incredibly powerful worldwide psychopathic cabal of self-appointed witchfinder generals, intoxicated on research grants, often tenured professors who will merrily destroy the career of any honest or professional scientist who examines their peer reviewed data and innocently remarks, "Eh, hold on here... something is not quite right with these findings..."

Borderline Personality Disorder (BPD) is a pharmaceutical industry/scientific and psychiatric con job conjured up as a method of determining prolonged disturbance of personality function in a person characterised by depth and variability of moods for which a pharmaceutical product is magically produced to 'cure' this mythical condition.

The diagnoses of BPD typically involves unusual levels of mood instability, black and white thinking, or splitting. The disorder often manifests itself in idealisation and devaluation episodes, as well as chaotic and unstable interpersonal relationships, self-image, identity, and behaviour, including a disturbance in the individual's sense of self. In other words, most of the same behaviours seen in psychopaths.

The BPD diagnosis ignores the remorselessness and high testosterone aspect of psychopathy, and with this one small edit a new disease was created by Big Pharma to sell a plethora of drug 'treatments'. Not to mention it became a golden ticket for many female psychopaths in particular who were no longer remorseless predators, but 'unfortunate women with a disease...'

Along with the reclassification of many female psychopaths as being Borderline Personality Disorder and the attendant horrors entailed for the rest of us, BPD is also being used to diagnose people who have nothing wrong with them other than mood swings or normal depression. Moody teenagers (is there any other kind?) are being diagnosed now as 'Borderline' and then fed truckloads of drugs by Big Pharma which is only too happy to sell them at colossal profits.

More disturbingly, BPD is a made-up disorder inspiring a multitude of articles and books, yet about which very little is known based on actual clinical research. In other words, the condition is completely fake and can be applied to just about anyone. It is a one-size-fits-all 'disorder' which covers endless numbers of human behaviours considered 'abnormal' by psychiatrists.

However, where BPD really shines is in courthouses worldwide where female psychopaths who may be accused of anything from staging fake kidnappings in order to have their terrified families (including their own young children) pay a huge ransom to their lovers, to female child/elderly abusers, con artists and serial bigamists, all now claiming to be 'unwell' with Borderline Personality Disorder with the result that many receive lenient treatment in the courts as a result. Gee, thanks, Big Pharma!

THE FEMALE PSYCHOPATH

Contrary to popular misconception, political correctness among mental health care professionals and active marketing by the Borderline Personality Disorder money machine, there are as many female psychopaths as males roaming the world. This notion of psychopaths being mostly male is reverse, *ad hoc* sexism. If there is equality between the sexes in all other aspects of life, then this equally applies to psychopathy.

For every male Pol Pot with his Western Intellectual 'education' demanding that Cambodian citizens be slaughtered in his killing fields to create a race of 'New People,' there is equally a female Madeleine Albright who, when informed on American TV that sanctions against Iraq which she ordered had led to the death of half a million children (more than died in Hiroshima), Albright replied, *"The price is worth it."*

The hormone testosterone is the key to recognising female psychopaths. They have the same incidence of elevated levels of the hormone as male psychopaths. Studies of non-disordered women indicate that higher testosterone levels are associated with increased sex drive, increased sexual activity and sexual attractiveness to men and as a result a desire to hold power over them. Vicious bullying and aggressive exploitation of non-psychopathic females in workplaces and organisations is also common with the pathology. Testosterone may also be related to the lack of parenting behaviour seen in many psychopathic women. Women with higher testosterone have been found to be less interested in motherhood, even when they have children.

Any man who has been in a relationship with one will attest to the above. Having been in the Punk-Metal and Goth scenes as a musician in my teens and early 20's, I can attest to the sexually aggressive, predatory, She Wolf female psychopathic archetype as being very real indeed. Not just in the music business, but in suburban communities and small towns all over the world.

In many cases, this is what makes female psychopaths so sexually appealing. Men will find themselves in bed with a female psychopath within hours of first meeting one. The sex can often be intense, even almost superhuman. The flattery will be amazing as well. Being called 'the most handsome man, and the greatest lover they ever had' just explodes one's ego into orbit, but it is all a tactic they have used with almost certainly hundreds of other men depending on their age.

TYPICAL FEMALE PSYCHOPATHIC TRAITS

- Unexpected sexual arousal
- Large clitoris
- Pronounced Adam's Apple (by female standards)
- Waking up in pools of sweat even in cool weather
- Somewhat unfeminine posture when viewed from behind (but this is not a hard and fast rule)
- Violent or sadistic sexual requests (wanting their nipples bitten hard, etc)
- Falling asleep and waking up instantly. Sleep and waking is instantaneous with all psychopaths
- Unexpected swing from idealisation of male partners to almost instant cold rejection leaving one feeling shattered, confused and with symptoms similar to Post Traumatic Stress disorder which can last from months to years

If you are a 'nice guy' you are more of a target — they will often remark how kind and nice you are. This makes you easy prey.

Most psychologically and emotionally mature men crave affection and loving sex. They have the desire to 'make love' and bond with their lover. But you will not get this with a female psychopath. You might get this 'love' as a performance for a while during the courtship phase, but sex will become almost robotic when the relationship is fully established and far less frequent (well, for you that is).

You will also find that the early sweet and loving kindness performance of the female psychopath will be interrupted now and again with a nasty and mean performance. Then a cycle develops where the frequencies of the nasty state increases — while the kindness state become less and less. Eventually, from the height of loving, idealisation and adoration the female psychopath obsessively showered you with in the early days, you will find yourself trapped in a negative, unloving and exploitative lifestyle not of your making.

You may in time not only find yourself no longer sleeping in the same bed as the psychopathic female, but you'll even be moved into the basement while she takes control of the rest of the house you are working hard to pay for. This will happen because you are a nice guy and you indulged her to avoid a fight, or hoping things would get better. You may even be feeling sorry for her as she is 'borderline..'

She will spread negative and false rumours about you to her friends while garnishing sympathy from her on-tap plethora of female pity enablers who believe every negative statement about you which she tells them. The female psychopath also generally befriends less attractive, overweight, 'frumpy' and unstylish women in order for the female psychopath to look more attractive when in their company. However, if the average 'hot' testosterone-packed female psychopath were to be removed from their highly selective female social network and placed among genuinely pretty or beautiful women, the female psychopath will then appear plain or 'hard-looking' in comparison.

If any men reading this have had a one night stand with a female psychopath, you will more than likely have had an enjoyable sexual experience, but there is a catch. Chances are you are one of hundreds of similar one-night stands, so do not fall for the female psychopath telling you she has fallen in love with you. It's only words.

You are nothing 'special' and there is every chance of contracting a STD from the event. So be careful.

You might also find your wallet a bit lighter in the morning when she has vanished and an unexpectedly huge credit card bill appears at the end of the month. Worse still, she may claim to be pregnant by you if she senses you can provide her with free food and accommodation for a while. Female psychopaths are as numerous, and operate under the same predator mindset, as male psychopaths.

THE "BENEVOLENT" PSYCHOPATHIC FATHER

In any household where the father figure is a psychopath he will be constantly alluding to *'how lucky his children are that he puts food on the table and clothes on their backs'*. A non-psychopathic father will just feed and clothe his children as a simple aspect of normal human behaviour and parental obligations, and won't demand his children *'worship his benevolence for keeping them alive'*. The psychopathic father will foster and enforce a form of distorted gratitude within his children that they are very lucky that he does not let them starve to death and it is only his goodness which prevents them from starving.

A psychopathic husband will openly state in public that *'my wife is very lucky to have me…'* implying that he allows her to live by not beating her to death. Tragically, the wife too often comes to believe this in time and will be grateful for her husband's 'kindness' towards her. She will tell others what a great man he is, when in reality she should be asking them to rescue her from a crazy lunatic.

It is also not uncommon with a psychopathic father to implement the silent treatment on a target child who is not 'playing the game' to the requirements of their deranged patriarchal self-glorifying agenda. This can happen if the child starts getting wise to the fact that the psychopathic father figure is not the glorious, infallible domestic hunter-gatherer godhead they view themselves as being.

When the psychopathic father suspects they are not unconditionally worshiped by the child, they will most likely perceive this as a threat or an attempt to 'usurp the throne'. The child then becomes a target of the psychopath and will thus be declared 'a liability' within the family structure and given the silent treatment, usually during the most emotionally sensitive and insecure stages of their teenage years when they are the most psychologically vulnerable. This sometimes leads to the distraught child turning to drugs or committing suicide, precisely what the psychopathic parent wanted when they implemented the silent treatment — particularly on a teenage son or daughter. The psychopath can then play the grieving parent in order to further their agendas with others in future.

PROTO-PSYCHOPATHS

Although it is incredibly rare for a female psychopath to end up in a relationship with a male psychopath, a socially inept female of low intelligence will actually go as far as enabling a male psychopath's most incredible demands in order to 'keep her man'.

Such was the case of Myra Hindley, half of the Moors Murderers double act, who — along with extreme psychopath Ian Brady — she kidnapped and sadistically murdered five children in and around Manchester, England between July 1963 and October 1965.

The victims were aged between 10 and 17, and at least four of them were sexually assaulted. During the trial, a tape-recording made by Brady of the pleadings of ten-year-old Lesley Ann Downey while she was being made to pose for pornographic photos was played in the courtroom. On tape, Myra Hindley can be clearly heard entering the room and demanding that the sobbing child *'Shut up.'*

Lesley Ann — addressing Hindley as 'mum' at Hindley's request, pleads with Hindley to let her go home. When presented in court, this evidence shocked the world at the time. The incredible lack of compassion Hindley, 'a woman, no less', showed towards a suffering child astounded and disgusted the British public.

There were two copies made of the tape. Brady was asked in court why he went to the trouble to listen to the whole thing and then to make a copy of it. *"Because it was unusual,"* was his reply.

This remark is typical of the psychopath who wonders why such a fuss is being made about the sexual torture and murder of a ten year-old child.

Hindley, when she heard the recording in the court, hung her head. When asked for her reaction upon hearing the tape, she said, *"I am ashamed."* Hindley was coming out of the spell which Brady had placed her under, and the full horror of her inhumanity caused by Brady's demands did, in my own personal opinion, genuinely impact upon her conscience.

Although Myra Hindley was to quite rightly spend the rest of her life in prison for her part in these horrific crimes, she constantly expressed remorse for her actions until she died at age sixty of cancer.

Ian Brady, being pure psychopath, never did this and predictably blamed Hindley for landing him in jail.

The proto-psychopath seems to have a strong sadomasochistic aspect in that they worship the authority figures above them (Ian Brady), while despising those they perceive beneath them (Lesley Ann Downey).

This is also commonly seen with women who are married to male psychopaths who then attack and abuse a target child within the family who reminds them of the psychopathic husband, and who also will be the child whom the psychopath feels the most threatened by — usually the eldest male child. Resentment of her psychological bondage to the psychopathic husband manifests in second-hand retaliation on the target child.

There is a subconscious programme put into their minds by the psychopathic husband that doing this would please them. The psychopath who has essentially mind-controlled his wife to beat this child will often then go on to call her a child abuser as he never laid a hand on the child. Incredible isn't it? Yet this goes on in suburban homes all over the world, hidden from public view every day. I have long wondered if the higher rates of teen suicide among young males in outwardly 'normal' families could be a result of this proto-psychopathic target child abuse.

The horrific saga of Myra Hindley and her psychopathic handler Ian Brady serves to remind us that even non-psychopaths can be brought under the psychopath's spell and perform the most horrific acts in order to appease them. They are still guilty, they still must be punished to the full extent of the law and these female (and male) proto-psychopaths are just as dangerous as the psychopath who put them under a trance in order to use them as an accomplice. However, they are not psychopaths if they come to accept and feel genuine remorse for their crimes. No matter how evil their criminality, no psychopath ever says "sorry" or feels remorse for their actions.

ARISTOCRATIC PSYCHOPATHS AND PROTO-PSYCHOPATHS

For their own self-serving agenda which has nothing to do with science, the elite are pathologically obsessed with Darwinian Evolution, which after 150 years still remains 'a theory' , in other words, 'a guess' — albeit the best one available thus far. This elite liked it so well, they made sure to immediately include it on school curriculums worldwide, even when the science behind it was at the very early stages of development and evaluation.

The body of Charles Darwin — a bigoted consanguineous aristocrat whose own elite family was ravaged by diseases and disorders caused by in-breeding — had hardly time to cool off before his tomb in Westminster Abbey was mobbed by secular pilgrims fanatically devoted to his 'theory'. His equally consanguineous half-cousin Francis Galton took up the family business with an eye towards continuing what Darwin decreed as 'the preservation of favoured races'.

Galton — who shared the same grandfather, Erasmus Darwin (the actual father of 'Natural Selection') — began implementing a scientifically-legitimised culture of genetic hierarchical mandates that would later become known as Racial Hygiene and Eugenics — the culmination of which were the lime pits and gas chambers of Auschwitz and Buchenwald.

This cultivation of proto-psychopathic behaviour in the children of elite and aristocratic families is nothing short of culturally-entrenched Dissociative Identity Disorder — utilising everything from being starved of emotional bonding with their mothers during infancy, right through the brutal private school systems and continuing on to military colleges and exclusive social clubs. The otherwise normal and emotionally healthy child will literally have its brain fragmented into compartmentalised alter egos in preparation to serve the elite agenda towards an ultimate unveiling of the carefully constructed proto-psychopathic personality when called upon.

During my late teens I was heavily involved in the animal rights movement, and among the activities we took part in was to protest fox hunting among the gentry and well-to-do. After witnessing these appalling and sadistic escapades close up, it soon dawned on me that the 'sport' of fox hunting actually is a psychological operation to mind-control young aristocrats and elites into the proto-psychopathic Dissociative Identity mindset.

The hunt would take place all day long and between the hounds barking constantly, the endless testosterone-fuelled bloodlust, the intense movement of the hunt party through the countryside to the din of wailing horns, even down to the riders dressed in almost day-glow red velvet finery — the visual and sensory impact of experiencing these hunts is overwhelming.

Now put yourself in the place of a ten-year-old boy or girl who is on this hunt with their parents for the first time. Not only is the intense sensory-overload of the day-long event a visceral assault on your psyche and senses. At the end of it all you witness an exhausted and terrified fox torn to pieces by frenzied dogs while still alive and howling in agony. Your father lifts you down from your horse and retrieving a piece of adrenaline-infused fox flesh, he then 'bloods' you with the still warm flesh by wiping it on your face. How could any child grow up psychologically balanced after an experience as deranged and twisted as this? Yet this is the culture that aristocrats defend and celebrate as noble and proof of their superiority over the rest of us. Prince Charles presumably did this to his own sons Harry and William just as his own father the Duke of Edinburgh did to him, and no doubt Harry and William will do the same to their own offspring. Is it any wonder how the world looked on at the Windsors (Saxe-Coburg and Gotha, if you please) during the funeral of Princess Diana, and were amazed at their casual detachment from the emotional impact of the tragedy while the BBC passed this off as 'stoic fortitude' and 'being strong for the nation'.

THE GAY COMMUNITY

This dynamic, diverse, affluent and primarily urban subculture represents a particularly lucrative hunting ground for male psychopaths as it feeds on their insatiable need for excitement, vanity and high-level, power-based sexual promiscuity. However, very few of the 'gay' psychopaths within this scene actually identify with homosexuality. As with all psychopaths, their *ad hoc* homosexuality is simply a tool to exploit and manipulate and not a natural expression of their true identity.

The gay community represents an exceptionally rich target environment for psychopaths to enter and exploit. These individuals can be compared to an invading army plundering this segment of society, taking full advantage of the sexual, financial and social opportunities the modern gay lifestyle presents to psychopaths. This is why many women who have been married to psychopaths are often shocked to discover that their ex-husband is now with a man.

The bed-hopping bi-sexual psychopath is just expanding his predatory portfolio and it has nothing to do with any real or meaningful embracing of their 'formerly self-repressed' homosexuality.

Psychopaths only ever 'come out of the closet' with their claws and fangs extended. The victims, be they the women they left behind, or the gay targets they are drawn to, will all be equally ravaged and devastated. This phoney 'personal liberation' utilised by the psychopath will allow them to play every sanctimonious victim card they can find to not only justify their actions, but make it seem heroic and noble. The reality is they are just opportunistic vermin who are forging a path of misery and ruin through the lives of anyone they can prey on, be they gay or straight.

The modern gay community in just about every Western country is almost exclusively composed of middle-class and above single men with a high level of disposable income. This would be very tempting to any male psychopath looking for enablers. Gay men want to be loved and settle down just as much as any straight person wants the same. Gay friends have expressed to me how difficult and emotionally risky looking for a long-term monogamous relationship within their culture can be as there are no end of manipulative individuals willing to declare their eternal love for them and then move on a few weeks later to someone new. This, as we have seen, is the cast iron benchmark of the overall psychopathic pathology — the idealising, then devaluing of people.

I suspect the overwhelming majority of these shallow 'heartbreaker' types within the gay community may well be psychopaths who have moved into their midst as they perceive that the narcissistic pickings are juicier. If gay men went back to being an impoverished, marginal community once more, no doubt the number of psychopaths in the gay community would massively decrease as these predators move on for more profitable conquests.

Psychopathic Clustering

A psychopath has no sexuality as such, any more than it can love. They have no real viewpoints or ethics either. They 'believe' in what you would like them to believe in (at first anyway). Psychopaths align themselves with belief packages and lifestyles simply as a lure or smokescreen. It is always like this with these chameleon predators. Again, it is 'just business' and whatever it takes to get them what they want is what they become. It is not just amongst marginal groups and sub-cultures such as gays, psychopaths move from scene to scene — new age groups, pop and dance scenes, you name it.

An old friend of mine was a former detective who worked in San Francisco as a community police officer during the 1960's. He once remarked how in the early days of the hippie scene it really was a case of 'peace, love and understanding'. There were good relationships between the police and the original pacifist hippies. 'Sweet kids' was the term he used to describe them. However, as soon as the hippie culture became mainstream he told me the city was literally invaded with all kinds of 'psychos' who simply put on a headband and stitched peace signs onto their jackets and moved into the Haight-Ashbury district of the city.

Before long, murders, rapes, robberies, suicides and other negative elements invaded the idealistic and peaceful hippie scene. This was due to the psychopaths moving into the scene who became 'hippies' in order to get the 'free love' and other personal gratification the counterculture offered. Subsequently — as with all psychopathic invasions — the underlying integrity and stability of the community descended into chaos and negativity. Psychopaths are never team players, though like individual flies they can form an *ad hoc* swarm when they detect fertile ground to gather upon and lay their eggs in.

HOMOPSYCHOPATH

Apart from sharing my lifelong experience with other people in the hope that victims of psychopaths can realise they are not alone and that we can gain from this experience, I also wrote this book as a warning. The world is in danger of being quite literally overrun by psychopaths and proto-psychopaths in positions of political, corporate military and scientific power.

For thousands of years, whether through the dynastic influence of royalty, governments or captains of industry, the world has been for the most part driven by the psychopaths at the very top — and it is becoming worse.

They are now on the verge of creating a world where only the powerful and influential psychopaths can prosper. The rest of us are to be essentially phased out and replaced with transhumanism and later posthumanism where a handful of elite aristocratic families and their agents are the only inhabitants of a world worked by organic robots who once had human ancestors but ended up being 'upgraded' to completely controlled cyber-slaves. Now you know why the latest robots are no more advanced than the awkward waddlers of the 1950's. Why bother developing robotics as a real science when all the psychopaths in control have to do is replace the parts of us which bother them with electronics and microchips?

Are you shocked in reading this? Well you shouldn't be. They make no bones about it. Even a casual Internet search will reveal that the same psychopathic social engineers running the show for over a century have been planning on destroying what makes you human. It is openly admitted in all their policy documents and many major corporations' future mission statements. Nothing to get too emotional about. Just business.

This is why it is vital that as many people as possible become aware of psychopaths and psychopathology as we are possibly on the brink of extinction. These think-tanks and globalist talking shops which meet in remote hotels and palaces to decide your future finally have the technological and logistical ability to begin to implement their transhumanist and posthumanist agenda. They may indeed be meeting to save polar bears from global warming, but their true aim is the destruction of something a psychopath cannot understand and considers a virus to be eradicated: *The human spirit.* Your soul. That which makes us who we are is not good for the psychopathic business and political agendas.

Human emotional life is a complete mystery to psychopaths, even as it provides them with the perfect blueprint on how to manipulate us.

If you have never taken LSD and someone who has is telling you what it is like, you find the experience so fantastically strange and bewildering. This is exactly how psychopaths react when normal people talk about their emotions and inner emotional lives.

The psychopaths who rule the world are no different in this respect than the ones you meet in the locals singles bars. Human emotional life is a pointless and absurd condition to them, and so they want to do away with it. This is why media is being used more and more to encourage and foster psychopathic behaviour in otherwise normal people. They are not making psychopaths out of non-psychopaths per se — they are manipulating otherwise decent people to emulate psychopathic traits and then to view these traits as the norm.

The entertainment industry is filled with this message, especially in pop music. When Lady Gaga parades around in a dress made from animal flesh it sends out a message to the millions of young impressionable minds that you are just a hunk of animated meat yourself. This is not by accident. This is not 'art'. Very real psychopathic individuals behind the scenes in music and entertainment are slowly altering your psychology in order to dehumanise you so that when the day comes to replace your free will, your human spirit and your soul with a microchip, you'll accept it, as you will have been conditioned by mass media to view your own humanity as just soulless meat.

The fashion industry with its size zero models, asexuality and flirtation with paedophile imagery is on the forefront of the psychopathic transhumanist agenda. Who are these fashion designers really? Where did they come from and why do they seem to all have the same agenda? These are questions you need to ask yourself constantly. Who gains from all this? Malcolm McLaren, former fashion designer and manager of the Sex Pistols, Adam and the Ants and Bow Wow Wow came right out when he stated in an interview with Simon Reynolds, *"I decided to use people, just the way a sculptor uses clay."*

Pornography also plays a huge part in human sexual degradation and dehumanisation. Individuals such as Hugh Hefner are presented as a lovable charming old uncle and not the trashy and sleazy peddler of pornography he actually is. *Playboy* has actively marketed their brand name to children in recent years in the form of school and fashion accessories for pre-teens. As an industry which has dehumanised women for decades now, the current trends for younger and younger porn actresses including 'MILFs' barely out of their teens, with silicone implants, Botox, and shaved pubic hair are one more step closer to a transhumanist society.

It gets even more worrying with the recent developments in sex toys for men. Artist Matt McMullen creates and markets disturbingly realistic female sex dolls under the brand name of RealDoll™ complete with orifices, real-to-the-touch skin and hair and with moving parts and programmable personalities. These sex dolls can cost up to $10,000 each and the demand is huge. Customers report having developed emotional bonds with their RealDoll™ after having had sex with them. One RealDoll™ owner had a customised one made in the image of his dead girlfriend. Another carries a picture of his doll around in his wallet as if it was his real wife and snuggles up with his RealDoll™ while watching TV.

Another realistic sex doll producer, TrueCompanion even supplies Frigid Farrah, who will spurn and resist sexual advances in order for her owners to rape her. What is truly unsettling is that much like the breast implants industry which became popular via the sex industry, will future generations of young women feel compelled to mimic increasingly realistic sex robots in order to get a real man?

These sex dolls also foster and legitimise psychopathic behaviour in men who purchase them as pretend sexual assault victims. The implications for society as a whole are worrying to say the least. Unless of course you are a transhumanist psychopath who sees this as a technological dream come true.

As I have mentioned throughout this book, the aim of the transhumanist movement is to remove human consciousness from the Earth except for a privileged few. A vital stage of their agenda is to create a bond between machines and humans so we accept them as equals firstly, and then as our 'natural' evolutionary replacements. This will be initially sold to us as robotic limbs and other organs for handicapped and disfigured individuals. These are noble and proper uses for such high-technology, but there will be an overall thrust in development in the coming years to 'upgrade' otherwise healthy individuals with implantable micro-chips and music players/phones which will be directly connected to the human brain.

Already an advertisement was transmitted into pedestrians who were walking down a New York street which they only heard in their minds as if it was God talking to them. This is why we must not allow marketing and advertising to make us rush to these products on impulse just because they are promoted as 'cool'. Always question, carefully consider and be cynical of everything marketed at you and especially your children. As a parent you also have a duty to protect your child's consciousness, individuality and personality as much as you are obliged to feed, clothe and put a roof over their heads.

Bear in mind that children who were six or seven years old during the turn of the millennium (at the time of writing this book) are now preparing to attend college. They have never known a world any different than the one we all inhabit now, with full body searches in airports and cities bristling with CCTV. For these young people, this is *The New Normal*. This is why it is vital for parents to help their children understand that things they see around them now were not always this way and why it is important for them to fully grasp that fact, to be clear about the freedoms we have all lost in the past decade and before, and the freedoms we stand to lose in the very near future.

The psychopathic elite thinks in terms of generations. They are patient. They are content to breed people like us out before implementing the final stages of their trans and post-human agenda.

Internet message boards and blogs are frequented by self-confessed psychopaths and the dominant theme that seems to be emerging is that psychopaths are ready to come out of the closet — in the same way homosexuals have done in the past. They seem to forget that homosexuals did not come out of the closet with some master plan to hurt and exploit other humans, or violate heterosexuals' human rights. Psychopaths more and more do see themselves as a new branch of humanity and we — the rest of us — are the new Neanderthals. They are ready to come out of their own closet and will be expecting the rest of us to accept them and then lay down while they exploit and destroy us in plain sight.

One can see how the media is so important in all of this. More and more 'role models' on television programmes are essentially psychopaths. They have no real humanity to them. Look how death is handled on TV soaps. When a long-term character on the show dies tragically they have five minutes of shock and then down to the pub for a pint. The profound impact of the loss of life for the individual — not to mention the family and friends — is barely touched upon. The widow is in bed with some new guy within a few days, talking about how good it feels to have sex again... this is the pure psychopathic mindset and it has been perniciously pushed on us in steadily-increasing measures since the 1960s via every medium.

How many people are capable of seeing the movie character James Bond for the psychopath he is? He kills dozens of humans and then has sex with women who are themselves killed while his semen is still warm inside them. Is he bothered? Of course not — there's plenty more beautiful young women for pre-death intercourse with our hero 007. Just business and good old-fashioned entertainment. Or so they tell us.

A mantra one often hears from the Social Darwinism faction is that anybody can become a psychopath in the right situations such as wars or the need to survive a disaster. Well, maybe in Hollywood movies about war and post-apocalyptic scenarios. The reality and evidence would suggest that the opposite is true. Military research and documents going right back to the Napoleonic wars are filled with the generals and military strategists being rather upset that the vast majority of troops do not enjoy killing each other in battle. Even more worrying for the psychopathic war junkies, troops in combat situations have been shown to do anything to avoid killing an enemy. It has been demonstrated time and time again that unless an officer is present, troops will not shoot at the enemy to kill them if they can possibly help it. If they do shoot, they will aim for the legs or deliberately miss. That's humanity for you and it is something about our nature we should cherish. It is also the one thing that psychopaths want to remove from us. Permanently.

PSYCHOPATHIC TECHNOLOGY

With US government grant money, William J Tyler of Arizona State University has developed targeted ultrasound technology to get over this problem of human decency and respect for life. His 'Helmet of Obedience' will be able to manipulate pain and motivational centres in the brain at a finer scale than even current magnetic stimulation. According to Tyler, "We look forward to developing a close working relationship with DARPA and other Department of Defence and U.S. Intelligence communities to bring some of these applications to fruition over the coming years, depending on the most pressing needs of our country's defence industries."

In December 2010, the Massachusetts Institute of Technology (MIT) published findings of a research program including tests that applied magnetic fields to a knot of nerve cells in the human brain known as the Right Temporal-Parietal Junction (RTPJ). Researchers found that when the RTPJ was disrupted with these magnetic fields, the electrical conductivity within this region of the brain was reduced and the test subjects were more likely to judge actions solely on the basis of whether they resulted in suffering, and not whether they were morally wrong in and of themselves.

After receiving a 500 millisecond magnetic pulse to the side of the head just behind the ears, volunteers delivered verdicts on various stories which were told based on outcome rather than moral principle. The subjects were shown to be unable to make moral judgments that require an understanding of other people's intentions. In other words, the subjects became temporarily psychopathic.

Although this study did not actually prove anything in terms of morality being purely a by-product of electro-brain chemistry, the MIT researchers did indeed demonstrate that technology can be used to switch off a person's sense of morality and empathy.

The US Air Force Research Laboratory's 711th Human Performance Wing updated a call for proposals in November 2009 that examine 'Advances in Bioscience for Airmen Performance.' Included in this document were proposed funding and research into technologies that can modulate an airman's emotional state. This included mind-altering drugs or biochemical pathway techniques. One would have to wonder about the kind of airman who would want his mind changed in order to kill and feel no terror during battle. In effect, the US Air Force wants technology to turn normal people into psychopaths at the touch of a button.

This kind of military development is very worrying and should be of great concern should it fall into the commercial sector. Which it inevitably will. Corporations would only be to0 eager to administer a pill which would rob their employees of their humanity in order to beat their competitors. Such techniques could also be used on the general population to desensitise them to having empathy for civilian victims of overseas wars. Can anyone honestly say that the same Big Pharma corporations who prescribe countless millions of psychotropic drugs to 'difficult' (read: *normal*) children in order to shut them up would not develop markets for a psychopathic pill? CompassionX, ExLove and UnRemorse anyone? I can see the tag line now; *"When Guilt is Holding You Back..."*

Don't say it won't happen.

Human free will and basic human morality is so disturbing to the psychopathic control grid that undoing our instinctual humanity is a major governmental concern these days. The European Union has recently funded the University of Bergen in Norway to create a website that collects people's opinions on three emerging techno-psychopathic technologies: biometric ID, human augmentation, and global tracking systems. The bureaucrats want to know why humans do not want to have their humanity taken away and then being turned into robotic slaves who question nothing and why our privacy and personal dignity is so important to us.

The European Unions' TechnoLife Project will present the objections of concerned citizens to EU policy makers *so they can then sell the transhumanist agenda in a direction that is more acceptable to the general population.* Taxpayer money is being spent by psychopaths obsessed with creating a transhumanist and posthumanist society to determine why humans are so fond of their free will and humanity. It simply beggars belief — but it is happening. This is how psychopaths view the rest of society: as problematic livestock to be stripped of its free will and humanity.

TIME TO WAKE UP AND SMELL THE BUSINESS PLAN

I would implore the readers of this book to please wake up and look around you and ask yourself if you are living in a world which is going in a direction which is good for the human race as a whole. Then ask yourself why. If you honestly investigate, you will always come across psychopaths of all races and ethnic persuasions pulling the strings behind the scenes in big business and government and very often in plain sight, in the public eye. The puppet masters are really out there and they are a fact.

Do not take my word for this alone. Research for yourself — think for yourself. Question media, science, politics, and do not blindly accept what is told to us as fact by authority figures, major corporations and organisations such as the World Bank, IMF, WHO, UN and other strategists of global public opinion. We all need to stop watching *Dancing with the Stars* and begin to look at the wider world with critical eyes and then start doing our homework. It will be the only thing which will save the human race from the psychopathic posthumanist agenda.

The good news is we will win. But not as a revolutionary movement. Not even as a collective. We do it by ourselves as individuals — transcending the destructive and degrading influence psychopaths have placed on our personal lives as well as psychopaths at the level of social control. We have to become *Consciousness Liberators* and we do that by reclaiming our sovereignty and psychological liberty through non-compliance with the psychopath control grid in relation to the psychopaths hell-bent on destroying the human spirit.

CAN PSYCHOPATHS SERVE A USEFUL PURPOSE?

In a 2010 paper in the journal *Evolution*, researchers at the University of Tennessee concluded that a pathological drive for power, to a limited degree, may actually be of benefit to society as a whole. What Professors Francisco Úbeda and Edgar Duéñez discovered was that the psychopaths maintain peaceful co-existence because they witnessed punishment being dished out to offenders. When it comes to a corrupt power structure the overall social integrity adapts to this corruption once it is limited. However, if the corrupt leaders of the society have too much power, then social order breaks down completely.

From this research we can assume that a little psychopathology can be a valuable asset in developing sensible legal and policing structures in order to protect the overall society. Due to a 'cause and effect' scenario whereby the psychopath's pathology implements a Pavlovian conditioning in relation to how victims and legal structures respond to the effects of psychopathology on society, it would seem to indicate that everything in nature — including psychopaths — are here for a reason.

Like it or not, the pathology has now been scientifically validated as an evolutionary impulse to force the rest of us to adapt in order to develop personal and social survival methodologies to overcome negative effects before they get out of control completely. As an example of this, the catholic church in Ireland essentially assumed the role of a paedophilic industry between the 1930s and 90s until the full horrors of its protection of paedophile priests became public knowledge. This eventually led to enacting laws to protect children, and later led to introducing gay rights, divorce and contraceptive legislation into Irish law, creating a more tolerant society for all. This probably would never have happened, or would have taken many more years to implement if the psychopaths in the Irish catholic church behaved themselves while they enjoyed so much power and influence in Irish society.

As I stated at the start of this book, psychopaths are the ultimate pawns in a game they can not possible win, *as long as we are wise to them and their predatory ways at all levels of society.*

Psychopaths can dodge and weave all they like, but once the average person wakes up and sees the control grid for what it is, it becomes a gift and there is nowhere left for the psychopath to hide.

The only real power the psychopath ever held was due to our ignorance, and they are presently finding it increasingly difficult to remain a hidden scourge in society.

Abject and
lost lay these,
covering the

flood

under amazement
of their

HIDEOUS

change.

from
Paradise Lost

John Milton

CHAPTER NINE

EMPATHY IS RECOVERY

S o here we are. We have reached the doorway to the labyrinth of the psychopath and the liberating rays of the restorative sun are bursting though the mouth of the tunnel and beckoning you towards the salvation and inner peace you have longed for. The dark inner centre of the psychopathic maze is now far behind you and the demon lurking in the shadows can no longer pull you back inside. You are free now to walk the final few steps to liberation. However, winning the war is one thing; winning the peace is another.

You have survived the labyrinth and on the way you have learned much about the pathology, along with the control and methodology of the psychopathic mindset. Your graduation is complete — now it is time to go to work on the next stage of your development, *the new you*. But you must remain vigilant that you are not hauled back into the abyss.

The psychopath commits a form of persona suicide when they decided you were surplus to their requirements. Most people in this situation are simply shocked and bewildered at how the psychopath they may have known for years is speaking to them and demonstrating the body language of a complete stranger, yet the psychopath can at any point in the future restore or reanimate this dead persona inside them if needed. They implement a kind of Lazarus rising from the tomb whereby the old persona they used to work you may once again be required.

However, as a former victim you must not fall for this repugnant 'undead' routine. The way you fully accomplish this is by taking the time to examine your own heart in order to ascertain what parts of yourself you felt were missing that the psychopath hooked into for their hold on your soul. Put more gently, you must be willing to *change*, to grow and discover how complete you are in yourself, and accept that relationships should enhance your experience rather than fill some part of you that you thought was missing.

The psychopath performs a persona suicide when they declare you obsolete, so why should victims continue to deal with them as if they are alive? The persona is dead — think of them as dead and buried. NO CONTACT EVER AGAIN is the key to attaining this state. Even if you have to deal with them via co-parenting your children you must consider the psychopath a ghost and not a living person.

One woman who wrote to me told me she made herself imagine she was smelling the odour of death when around her psychopathic ex when he came to collect the children. She said after a while the psychopath became increasingly less arrogant and smug around her, eventually acting unsettled and perturbed. He ultimately gave up and left the country without informing anyone and hasn't been heard of since.

They know when your energy is no longer available to them and — scared this may rub off on others around you — they make a run for it to search for a new source of emotional energy to feed on and decent souls they can manipulate and exploit. The reality is their inevitable crash into oblivion comes another step closer. They still don't get why if they had been kind, considerate and empathetic they may have avoided their social and economic decay. It's always someone else's fault and not theirs — right to the very last breath exiting their dying bodies.

Look After Yourself

People in relationships with psychopaths often have repressed immune systems. One of the things victims notice is that after they have overcome the mental trauma they suddenly feel healthier than they have in years. Their overall health is actually slowly improving, while their mental and intellectual facilities return with a vengeance. The toxic maelstrom the psychopath engulfed you in is purging itself as a true form of healthy energy — real life-force — suffuses every cell of your body.

Not just your body is restoring itself, but your mental health is being rejuvenated too. It is almost like your brain is akin to a falsely-convicted prisoner being pardoned and released from jail. Your intellect in the post-psychopathic abusive/manipulated state seems sharper, more innovative and fired-up. All the intellectual abilities which the psychopath nullified in you over time in order to mind-control you more effectively begin to make a comeback.

Victims of psychopaths are usually not even aware of how unhealthy they were until they are finally clear of the psychopath. Common 'mysterious' conditions which survivors find themselves recovering from include:

- Itching and Rashes
- Lethargy
- Irregular Bowel Movements
- Hyper Vigilance
- Nightmares
- Sleep disturbance
- Fatigue
- Anxiety
- Abdominal Pain
- Lack of Ambition
- Problems with Concentration
- Impaired Memory
- Asthma
- Low Self-Esteem/Self-Loathing

CONFUSION

Many people have been deeply affected by their time in the labyrinth to a greater degree than they initially suspected. This is indicative of how little attention they have paid to themselves while under the influence of the psychopath. Survivors often convey to others a sense or feeling that their life energy and a large portion of their soul has been taken by the psychopath.

This is very real and anyone who says it isn't is either very lucky to have never been near a psychopath, or are a psychopath themselves. They are also denying a basic underlying principle of the universe: that everything is energy and every kind of evolution from the grand cosmic scale to the most microscopic single-celled organism is all energy interacting with other forms of energy, creating novelty and new trajectories of development. Your own personal psychological and spiritual growth works exactly the same way.

We are all made up of energy. That, and consciousness is all we are. Quantum physics — the science underlying this fact — remains the most intensely-tested and retested of all scientific principles. The evidence is beyond doubt that we are pure energy and the material world is a manifested interpretation of sub-atomic particles from which we form our worldview. This includes the psychopaths who come into our lives. We created our connection to them and we can un-create it, too. That's how powerful we are.

This is the crux of, and the underlying message of this book: We have to come to terms with whatever 'need' existed in our worldview and in our psychological, emotional and spiritual makeup that convinced us *we were somehow incomplete as souls*, thus attracting the psychopathic experience into our lives.

The good news is by understanding and coming to terms with these aspects of our psychology and spiritual nature we can successfully overcome the after-effects of the experience, but even more important, become immune to all psychopaths because of our hard-won awareness of what they are and how they function in society. Isn't that the best news of all?

Once we understand the rules of the game, we are no longer pawns. We are the kings and queens on the chessboard and the psychopath will literally just leave the game. Checkmate.

FAREWELL MY PSYCHOPATH—
HELLO THE REAL ME

Those who ignore the impact of psychopaths on individuals and society as being a very real, personal, social, financial and political problem — if not the single greatest danger to the human race's future survival — will forever shake their heads in anguish at behaviours they either cannot come to terms with and or will forever rationalise away until it eventually destroys them. Psychopaths are all business and go about their schemes in an almost pragmatic manner, but their main currency is the emotional and psychological rape of others.

We should not feel sorry for psychopaths EVER. As we have seen, feeling pity for them is one of their main hooks for luring in unsuspecting, caring people. They are not innocent victims of illness or disorders.

There is only so much life energy in a psychopath and it is nearly all being used up by their devious intent. It is no wonder so many of them have endless medical complaints, dead eyes, unnerving stares, annoying habits, crazy, wild handwriting, the legendary weird sleep patterns and an inability to produce any kind of technical document or schematic — let alone read them.

The psychopathic biological machine is far from perfect — hence their emotional vampirism — gaining 'rushes' from their 'wins' and carefully crafting scams which rob us of our energy via every encounter including one-night stands to systematic financial destruction and political control. The flesh, blood and bones of a psychopath is a shell. Inside there is no man, nor woman, just a predator who can be anything we need them to be, for as long as it serves the predator.

YOUR PERFECT HUMANITY
IS NON-NEGOTIABLE

When a psychopathic consciousness enters the human body at the moment of conception they find it hard work to keep the biological host operating with the same efficiency as a human consciousness/

soul does. It is akin to a young teenager stealing a car, but not being a good enough driver to work the controls properly. In the case of psychopaths, the full skill set needed to operate inside the human skin they cloak themselves within are simply not all there.

This is what makes them easy to spot when you are aware of their bio-behavioural idiosyncrasies. This defectiveness of the psychopath is being projected onto the rest of humanity as a whole and may well explain in a broader socio-psychological sense this transhumanist rush to have us all 'upgraded'.

If one watches video interviews with the main proponents within the transhumanist movement, it becomes almost laughingly apparent that they are hardly the kind of people who have personalities which will set the world on fire — certainly not with any erudite social sparkle they may have.

Yet these classic, socially inept, emotionally vapid uber-nerds who can barely string a sentence together, nor make proper eye contact are the ones who have declared human beings as a defective, obsolete species which needs to be urgently upgraded to soulless robots for future industrial production and the service industries — classic psychopathic projecting, imposing their own personal shortcomings upon the rest of humanity. This is why we must resist these individuals at all cost and with the same steadfastness as we resist any psychopathic control grid; be it in a relationship, or of a political, commercial, economic or scientific origin.

Let no one, no corporation or no government switch off your humanity in order to make their own business models run smoothly or be more profitable.

Brain (Power) Drain

One of the main problems psychopaths have with operating a human body is extreme difficultly with their electrical system. This is most apparent in their brain and nervous system functioning.

Dr Robert Hare, PhD, during his research on psychopaths using CAT scan technology, proved beyond a doubt that the brain of a psychopath stores information in a scattered manner, instead of in the normal partitioned regions within the cerebral cortex. Part of this involves the lack of vital neurotransmission functioning. Information is then scattered all over the entire psychopathic brain and results in a longer than normal amount of time for the psychopath's brain to retrieve and process information.

Their waking brain functions resemble the activity of a normal person in a light sleep. No matter how educated or not the psychopath is, there is simply not enough of the brain switched on in order to be truly creative, innovative, talented and seamlessly dynamic in social situations. Certain parts of their brain functions have to be sacrificed in order to maintain their devious agendas and fake personas. Interestingly enough, the brain of a normal person goes into a light sleep mode similar to the psychopath's usual state while we are watching TV, suspending critical thinking, making the normal brain more inclined to impulsiveness and susceptible to suggestion — just in time for the commercials...

Now think back to when you were in a relationship with a psychopath and how the crazy-making seemed to always involve the psychopath's sheer incompetence in performing the most basic technical or domestic tasks, while at the same time talking down to you as if you were the imbecile and the moron. The psychopath in the middle of a project can suddenly switch to something else for no apparent reason and completely out of the blue, their previous 'vital, highly important' project discarded as though it never existed to begin with.

The psychopath may have also constantly made weird irritating noises, used bizarre, obnoxious phrases and tones, spoke with a cartoon style voice, mispronounced words in an annoying infantile manner, referred to themselves in the third person, as in, *"Mr Slick thinks..."* and *"John Franklin is not the kind of man to do..."* and be incredibly socially rude by belching loudly, lighting a cigarette in a non-smoker's home without asking if it is OK first, or sneezing intensely like a crazy scream.

One psychopath childhood victim I knew told me he used to have his head placed under his father's buttocks while the father passed wind in the child's face. The child was then laughed at and ridiculed. The psychopathic father would then encourage the mother and siblings to join in the humiliation and mocking of the child (developing proto-psychopaths). When the child broke down after one humiliation too many the father started calling the ten-year-old child *'a queer who is not a real man... '* This is how the unchallenged psychopathic parent cultivates absolute control of the family unit within a home. They will do it to your country, too, if they can get the power — airport naked body scanners being a prime example .

Can you recall the psychopath's arrogance and grandiosity as they claimed to be an expert on this and that, then proceeded to 'upgrade' your computer, 'soup up' your lawn mower or 'develop a business proposal' that was surreal in its total incomprehensible, scatter-brained stupidity?

Want to see what the political version of such pathology is like? Then look no further than the American NeoCon's *Project for the New American Century*, a manifesto so divorced from reality that if it wasn't responsible for the deaths of millions of innocent people around the world would be considered a script to a *Monty Python* sketch.

When the psychopath gets bored with their latest master plan to improve something that was fine to begin with (very often you), they walk away from your now broken computer, destroyed lawn mower, ethnically-cleansed nation. The psychopath will then talk down at you as if it was your fault for not validating their visionary genius, hence why it didn't work out... sound familiar?

In any relationship with a psychopath the victim is always the more intelligent, insightful, educated and clever partner, but the psychopath will campaign as though their life depended on it to convince you that you are the liability, you are a write-off and you are the dead weight holding them back. This is the result of a grandiose halfwit psychopath who is only good for one thing and one thing only: *Being a manipulator*. Apart from that, they are bullies, parasites and imbeciles and they are jealous of all the things you are and can feel that they can never be or experience.

Even the often enjoyable testosterone-driven sex life of your early encounters with the psychopath will suddenly vanish once the relationship has been established. These once great bedroom performances still exist — someone else is being manipulated with them now. You are no longer in the game. As soon as the wedding ring was on your finger or you signed over the deeds to your property, the psychopath is off doing the same to the next sucker. Same rule applies for the elaborate romantic dinners the psychopath wooed you with. Somehow that was replaced with you ordering pizza a long time ago, and eating it alone.

Can you see how on every level psychopaths are another sub-species of humanity? The Homopsychopath archetype in media is the engine which drives our social and relationship model these days. Nevertheless, they remain a deeply inferior sub-species due to their badly functioning neuro-electrical systems. They cannot get away from this no matter how powerful they become — even when 'leader of the free world'.

The Homopsychopath is a lemon at the end of the day. For all their enjoyment of calling other people idiots and morons, or their new favourite term of abuse, *tards* — the psychopath has the most inferior brain of any hominid, and I would include most species of monkeys and apes in this. Primates know what love and bonding is and why it is important to their overall survival. This is why in the end, we will win and psychopaths will lose. We are the truly wise ones. The kind of deep-rooted emotional, spiritual and intellectual wisdom that can only originate from the rich experiences of the human condition — a wisdom so powerful that via its gestation within the human soul it waits to manifest into the hearts of decent men and women.

You Have a Right to Remain Human

This may seem like a dark time in human history. The psychopaths are almost at their endgame of complete domination of global society, but that dam of good old-fashioned human love and compassion is building up and the cracks are already forming in the barrier which the psychopaths have used to wall up our collective human potential. The unstoppable tsunami of human decency and collective human potential for good is now a perceivable torrent. Psychopaths know this. That's why they fill our movies, TV screens and newspapers with stories of the most debase and appalling aspects of humanity (which they are the root cause of) in the hope that we as humans continue to hate ourselves and eventually come to think of as *The New Normal*. They continually gaslight and use projection techniques to destroy our personal, social and community self image.

For decades, nature documentaries have all had the underlying subtext that human beings (except for wealthy big game safari and aristocratic fox hunters, that is) are a danger to furry animals and we all should hate ourselves as a result. TV programmes about meerkat colonies are designed to make you forget having a sense of community, bonding and closeness with our human neighbours and seek to replace this with empathy for a TV meerkat colony instead while we sit back and hate ourselves for being 'horrible, destructive humans'.

When the Duke of Edinburgh, Prince Phillip, was killing large animals for sport in Africa it was known as 'big game safari.' Now this same absurd individual is one of the leaders of the World Wildlife Fund (WWF) and refers to the practice as 'illegal poaching' when Africans do it. These Africans are forbidden to enter nature reserves — some as large as England and now re-branded as 'conservation areas' — while African cities become more and more crowded.

On the other hand there are endless shark and other 'Killer Animals' shows on these 'educational' cable networks which preach another underlying subtext that these efficient killers and predators are noble and beautiful. A shark is just a shark doing its natural sharky thing — but when it is used as a metaphor for the psychopath in the context of a TV documentary, then you can see the agenda. They are the ones pushing the 'kill or be killed' notions. Most humans I know just want an easy life and not have to hurt anyone to get it.

The Utopian Psychopath: Beware of Geeks Bearing Gifts

One psychopathic mainstay that has been with us since the time of Plato's *The Republic* is the super wealthy but socially-inept psychopath who uses their money and family profile to 'repair' or 'improve' the rest of the human race who do not live up to the psychopath's notion of what a proper functioning society is. These personality types — from playing with models of buildings and toy people as children — failed to realise that the real people of this world are not made of injection-moulded plastic to be placed within model 'cities of the future' where they will be forced to conform to the utopian grand vision.

The utopian psychopath on his mission to save the world while containing the human race within communities of the future is single-minded in their desire to design and control sci-fi inspired cities, megalomaniac concepts and soulless inhuman, unnatural environments for us to be herded into. There we will be numbered and micro-chipped, all our comings-and-goings continually monitored, studied and measured in the pursuit of increasingly efficient and cost-effective ways to control us. We will be expected to relish being totally at the mercy of the machine community while video cameras inside our homes show the rest of the world what 'model' citizens we have become.

We will be kept up to date with the latest medications which will be injected into us during our chemically-induced sleep so we do not have to bother with developing an old-fashioned natural immune system. All our earthly imperfections and troublesome individuality will be medicated and routined out of us. Then, upon fulfilling 'the great work' — our utopian psychopath will sit back and lose interest in their perfect society, then move on to something else. We will then be left to rot as the infrastructure collapses into neglect and ruin.

From Jim Jones' People's Temple, in 'Jonestown,' Guyana, to the First Five-Year Plan of the USSR, to Mao's social-political programs, such as the Great Leap Forward and the Cultural Revolution, from the English Enclosure Act of the 12th century to the various planned communities of today; the psychopathic hunger is to pen the humans in and make them slaves for their utopian grand megalomaniacal visions. If millions are displaced, impoverished or murdered to make this happen then so be it. If people's psychological wellbeing, emotional richness, creative awareness and individuality can be just turned off by a centrally-controlled computer via an implanted microchip, then better still. No more messing about with mass graves and low-level psychopaths doing the whipping and manning the machine gun towers. Not cost-effective, you see.

A WORD OF CAUTION

Before you run off to be connected up to the central computer from your domestic housing pod, you might want to know about someone who had notions about containing the bacteria known as human beings, the completely insane and psychopathic Irenee DuPont, one time head of General Motors and Du Pont industries. Inspired by Hitler's principles, DuPont obsessed over the aims and policies of National Socialism from the 1920s on.

So enchanted with Hitler's notions of a Master Race that in September 1926 while addressing the American Chemical Society, he advocated a race of futuristic supermen, to be upgraded by injecting DuPont chemicals into them to transform them into improved humans to rule the world. DuPont also used General Motors money to finance an organisation known as the Black Legion to prevent GM workers from unionising, which he saw as a barrier to his chemically-enhanced utopian social order. Black Legion members wearing hoods and robes with skull and crossbones motifs fire-bombed union meetings, sometimes beating shop stewards to death.

DuPont gives one a perfect insight into the wealthy psychopath and the lengths they can go to in order to attain their utopian perfections. However, this same mindset can also be seen today among many college professors who have signed up to similar notions of a perfected, trimmed-down humanity.

Many of their conferences and talking shops are highly-funded, slick events which attract some of the biggest names in politics, media and science, all of whom enthusiastically pontificate about population reduction and implanting humans with computer chips — naturally not applicable to them, of course. The often infantile hollering and standing ovations from fawning academics often comes across as completely bizarre. Many of these individuals really do see themselves as the chosen earthly gods upon this planet with every right to make all the decisions that we 'useless eaters' must live and die by. Their detachment from the sheer inhumanity and spellbinding megalomania of their often surreal proposals to 'save the world' are incredibly elitist and ruthlessly narcissistic — and all done with a cheer and high-fives.

The issue is not that the audiences of these events are all psychopaths (although some most certainly are — others are brainwashed and research grant-drunk academic proto-psychopaths who have lost the run of themselves) but that many people who are highly educated these days appear to have only learned how to unconditionally defend authority figures and the *status quo*. This may go some way to explaining the collapse of interest in those formerly studying for a science degree in recent years. What idealistic person today, interested in becoming a scientist and lit up with the pure fervour of discovery and wonderment would want to hand over their entire working lives to the likes of the military-industrial complex, Big Pharma or the Rockefeller Foundation?

Wisdom and true enlightenment are not part of the mainstream educational journey and probably never have been. Matters not if we are dealing with a population-culling psychopath with a PhD who is spewing platitude-filled word salad — the party line seems to be, *he has a PhD and therefore he cannot be argued with…* Matters not if he is a crazy megalomaniac; his opinion is akin to law. This is a very unhealthy mindset as these academics are subject to the same follies and pathologies as all humanity and some will be psychopaths, driven by their own need to be adored in a sanctimonious fiesta of self-righteous backslapping grandiosity.

A highly-educated individual is not immune from being a psychopath or being an indoctrinated proto-psychopath employed to defend the edicts of 'infallible science' or more worryingly, social engineering. We should not automatically believe everything we are told to believe by a scientist for no other reason than that 'they are a scientist,' rather, we should consider all the information presented to us, do our own research and consider the full range of possibilities.

Many of these 'celebrity' scientists who may have expertise in one discipline, are increasingly being called upon by mass media/ governments to give their viewpoints on non-scientific issues and often with the most bizarre results — such as when Michio Kaku made the incredible and disgraceful accusation during a TV interview that people who question authority and the *status quo* are 'terrorists'.

Mahatma Gandhi, Rosa Parks, Crazy Horse, Monet and the Impressionists, Steve Biko, Mozart, John F. Kennedy, Lech Walesa and indeed Galileo Galilei would be deemed 'terrorists' using Michio Kaku's yardstick to quantify who is and isn't a danger to the *status quo*, yet the mainstream media let him get away with these shocking comments because *they agree wholeheartedly with them*.

Professor Kaku demonstrates how when it comes to issues beyond their own expertise, in his case Theoretical Physics, scientists are the last people we should be listening to.

Michio Kaku comes across as a decent man who means well, but when such people are employed as promoters of a psychopathic control system by adding their academic credential weight to the sometimes pernicious agenda, they can be very dangerous indeed — especially if they do not possess the same skills of a true polymath such as the late Carl Sagan, who often cautioned people to be aware of even his own speculation.

Science alone does not have all the answers, just as much as religion does not provide true wisdom and knowledge — even though more and more we are being encouraged to align ourselves with this concept of 'Scientism' as an unquestioned dogma. This 'my way or the highway' approach is pure pathology and is the bench-mark of the psychopathic totalitarian mindset.

I have found time and time again that most of the psychopaths I have encountered were the most ardent and smug defenders of science, even though these individuals had no real understanding of the scientific principle beyond the 'what he said' level of un-derstanding and insight. Psychopaths are lazy. They do not really study, they merely carry around certain books as props to make themselves appear learned.

Often this *'I am a man/woman of science and truth'* persona of the psychopath was simply to add some intellectual superiority to their public image to hide the fact they actually were clueless. Do not allow these psychopaths in media, government or in your homes to impose their belief package on you — be they secular or otherwise. It is a sham, a pose and is also a dangerous road to travel when proclaiming that every scientist who ever lived is as pure as the driven snow. We should not completely discard the imagery of the quack doctor or mad scientist either, because such individuals really do exist.

The notorious UNABOMBER Ted Kaczynski was accepted into Harvard University at the age of 16, where he earned an undergrad-uate degree, and later a PhD in mathematics from the University of Michigan. He became an assistant professor at the University of California, Berkeley at age 25. Then he started making bombs and killing innocent people in order to save the planet. Now where this gets very interesting is his manifestos are almost identical to the current depopulation fetish among intellectuals and college pro-fessors.

Ted Kaczynski's population reduction plan was implemented in an immediate 'hands-on' manner, whereas the pontificating psy-chopathic academics prefer mass sterilisation and forced abortions rather than pipe bombs. However, the same psychopathic un-derlying desire to slaughter humans so they — the elite educated class — can take over the planet and live as gods among pure na-ture is still what drives them — as it did the UNABOMBER.

All we humans are, ultimately, to these utopian psychopaths, is nothing more than cheap labour and a future source of fertilizer for their organic Edens.

Normal human beings do not have a desire to align the human condition within the social model of the bee or the worker ant. The defining system of management of every utopian concept, including the New Towns - brutalistic high-rise public housing of the 1950s and 60s, were all deeply-rooted elite psychopathology and social engineering based on an assumption that most humans who are not of a certain pedigree are wild animals — out of control, and needing to be locked up in a zoo and watched. All 'planned communities' are an expression of someone else's pathology at some point along the conceptual chain.

The utopian psychopath claims to care about nature and then wants to save the world from the impact of humans. What is most telling about this viewpoint is that humans are not considered natural or part of nature by the psychopathic control grid. Nature to them is plants, animals, scenery and other aristocratic psychopaths with a few select servants. In all their grand utopian vision the underlying subtext is always *to remove the humans.*

First item on the transhumanist and posthumanist agendas: make us into slave robots for the psychopathic elite, those they need to serve them in their glorious posthumanist future. Humans have no place in this future techno-psychopathic world view. We are the plastic toy people who are to be thrown into the recycle bin when we have served our usefulness.

So the next time some billionaire aristocrat or one of their paid-off scientists comes up with an idea to improve the human race and starts pulling out the models of utopian cities and efficiently-managed societies, ask yourself who really gains from this? Them? Or me and my loved ones, my society and humanity as a whole?

They will try to ridicule you with statements such as, *'Well, some people still believe the world is flat...'* or, *'Do we go back to living in caves...?'* Do not be intimidated by this tactic. Individuals who use such phrases are very often psychopaths or propagandists for psychopaths putting you in a position where you have to defend your intellect so that any chance of a meaningful debate is destroyed. It is no different than when a psychopath boyfriend remarks, *"You think too much. Now go make my dinner..."*

PSEUDO-INTELLECTUAL PSYCHOPATHS AND THE RATIONAL STRAW MAN

Pseudo-intellectualism coupled with totalitarianism is not science; it is fascistic bullying and in the case of many of these 'de-bunker' bloggers who invoke science during their straw man tactics, they are often intellectually-posturing psychopaths, sometimes paid by private and public agencies to de-rail any opinion which is not good for business or government policy.

In a *New York Times Magazine* investigation in 2011, Jake Crosby uncovered that one site, *Science Blogs,* started up a 'nutrition' blog called *Food Frontiers,* paid for by PepsiCo without any disclaimer being issued. This caused a mass exodus of twenty bloggers from the website when the blog's corporate agenda was exposed.

There was a time when genuine science bloggers once had credibility in the eyes of many; now they are increasingly viewed as pseudo-intellectual prostitutes for the exclusive benefit of powerful corporations, or their own personal egos, at the expense of environmental and public well-being. Psychopaths trying to look clever and/or making a quick buck for themselves in the name of 'rational science', of course, in much the same way Stanley Milgram test subjects 'killed' an innocent man with electrical shocks in order to prove their loyalty to the authority figure.

IS YOUR GOD A PSYCHOPATH?

- Does your god expect you to worship him and only him?
- Does your god punish you for questioning his motives even when you don't mean to?
- Does your god seem to have more than a passing interest in encouraging sectarian tensions for his own benefit?

- Does your god have a history of rubber-stamping genocide?
- Does your god relegate women to second-class status?
- Does your god love you one minute and then punish you the next?
- Does your god claim that he alone represents your spiritual salvation?
- Does your god come with a strict rule book?
- Does your god enjoy owning large real estate in prime city centre locations while having no source of income?
- Does your god suffer from Multiple Personality Disorder?
- Does your god tell you one thing and then do another?
- Does your god like to be referred to as 'the Supreme Godhead,' 'Lord,' 'King of Heaven,' "The Almighty,' 'Infallible,' etc?

The purpose of this list of questions above is not designed to attack or mock any reader's personal religious views or beliefs. I strongly consider that having a sincere personal spiritual outlook is vital in transcending the effect of psychopathic exploitation of the self and society at large. I would also make the point that atheists are at an extreme disadvantage when going through a psychopath survivor recovery scenario. This is also why I believe that the radical atheism of recent years has been promoted for this very reason; to rob people of their relationship with their higher selves in order to make them more readily accepting of the psychopathic Transhumanist and Posthumanist scientific/corporate agenda of the elites. Destroying the human soul is good for business and makes government control much easier.

Hence why the same people who tend to worship the likes of Richard Dawkins are also the most devoted to their deluded notion that the world is run by wonderful, altruistic people who love humanity, the environment and always do what's best for them. Personally, I consider this radical atheism a secular religion which generally attracts the same fanatical and intolerant personality types that any Islamic terrorist leader of today or pope of the Middle Ages would be only too delighted to have in their respective camps. Psychopaths, for the most part, adore atheism (even when they are clerics) and use it to exploit people as much as religious charlatans do.

I am pointing out, how with the Psychopath God list that you may have been primed by the autocratic, authoritarian political structures of all organised religions, from the Judeo-Christian-Islamic tradition to Hinduism to Buddhism — all the 'rulebook' religions. God doesn't need middle men other than to keep religion in business. Your god wants a personal relationship with you. A truly loving god is not a psychopath and will not impose judgement and rules upon you.

HEADLINES, SPIN AND BUZZ WORDS

I also cannot stress enough how important etymology is in relation to this subject. Words have power to create and destroy as well as enchant and inspire. As I stated at the beginning of the book, this is why I use the term 'psychopath' to name this pathology, as the word has a powerful negative connotation which softer terms such as 'narcissist' fail to convey. You cannot soften or water down the negative and toxic imagery which the term 'psychopath' stirs within your mind. The term 'narcissist' can seem in some contexts as almost romantic, conjuring images of pre-Raphaelite paintings of self-obsessed dandies pondering their reflections in idyllic lily ponds — hence why I avoid the term and psychopaths champion it.

Words and their meanings have far deeper consequences upon our psychology than most of us realise. Deeper meanings are often hidden within at first glance — mundane everyday words, terms and phrases. We have become a linguistically-ignorant society compared to the ones our grandparents and great-grandparents inhabited. One only has to look at letters written by working class people in the 19th century to realise this. Their letters and personal diaries are often carefully-crafted and eloquently expressed compared to the predictive text level of 'literacy' prevalent in society today.

In tandem with this we must also educate ourselves to become symbol-literate. We are constantly being given metaphors and allegories, often blatantly, via works of advertising and other visual and aural stimulation. This has been used for both good and sinister motives — from the deeply moving sense of emotional enchantment which passes over us when viewing the brush strokes of a Monet painting in a public art gallery to the crass corporate psychopathic subliminal messages which are doing tremendous damage to the human psyche as a whole, along with our spiritual and intellectual rape by propaganda and organised religion.

From the earliest artists moving red ochre across a granite cave wall where no natural sunlight penetrated, to the current Hollywood directors with their armies of actors, movie technicians, computer-generated visions and illusions, this has all been and still remains mind-control. In the past, art was used to enhance the human spirit. In terms of present day mass entertainment it is being utilised far too frequently by psychopaths to decay it.

A writer, when he or she creates a word, they *spell* the word. When you spell a word in the sentence, you literally are doing just that — *casting a spell.*

How often have we heard the phrase, *the pen is mightier than the sword*? How many individuals, organisations and even entire countries have been destroyed based on words *spelled out* on a page in the form of a satire, propaganda or manifesto? The psychopathic control grid has been putting all of us under a spell which has us believing that humans are powerless, vile, a pollutant on the planet and increasingly, that we are obsolete and need to be removed or replaced.

That violence and ruthlessness are sexy. That war is noble and 'kicks ass'. That murderous video game is just harmless entertainment. *'Hasn't messed up my kids!'* parents say, and then they wonder why ten years later they return home from the Middle East in coffins draped with flags. Hollywood, news and mass entertainment is pure psychopathic propaganda on a multitude of levels as scripts of TV shows and movies are handed on down from on high — and I am not talking God here.

Psychopathic marketing and mind-control is everywhere one looks. One of the benefits of having survived a psychopathic relationship is that you never see the world with the same eyes again. The same psychopathic techniques which were used on you at a one-on-one level you start to notice all around you as you awaken from *the spell.*

Are the popular series of books with titles such as *A Complete Idiot's Guide to…* and *This and That for Dummies* that claim to give you knowledge concerning a certain subject really respecting your intellectual ability? Or are they subliminally destroying your sense of self-worth by declaring you an 'idiot' or a 'dummy' in such a jovial, glib manner that you become dependent on these books to learn about the world due to the fact they have trained you to believe you are a moron? Think about it. You are being deeply, personally insulted when you purchase such books.

The fact that these titles sell in their tens of millions demonstrates just how entrenched this intellectual low self-esteem is among society.

How did this happen? Classic psychopathic tip-toe style and it is great for business. What works for the psychopathic parent destroying his children's self-esteem works for the marketer, advertising executive and major media player too.

POSITIVE THOUGHTS PRODUCE POSITIVE RESULTS

"Life's a bitch and then you die…"
"You can't fight City Hall…"
"Shit happens…"

How many times during your life have you heard one of the above expressions? In the course of an average week, it is possible to hear them all and many other similarly negative statements from others around you. What is the purpose of these comments? How many times have you looked back at your own life and thought to yourself, *'If only I had made this or that choice...'* or, *'What was I thinking back then?'* The last statement says it all; not only were you not *thinking,* you were *not feeling.* Or you were surprised by your *intuition* when in the early stages of being gaslighted by a psychopath you suppressed this internal warning bell. You owe it to yourself from now on to never let this happen to you ever again.

If you have a friend, co-worker, relative or an entire community/ society being gaslighted by a psychopathic situation, you must interject and explain what is being done to them. You are now a *Consciousness Liberator* whether you realise this or not. You have no choice. Many people who survived deeply psychopathic relationships want to write books so they can help others. There are far too many lambs waiting to be slaughtered when all they lack is knowledge of who the butcher is and how he operates.

Most people have no original thoughts or opinions of their own. They may think they do, but if they were to ask themselves what they really believe which was not planted in their minds by external sources they would most likely be stumped. This is how conditioned we have become to being mind-controlled — it makes the street level psychopath's job so much easier when it comes to targeting us as individuals. We have already been softened up.

All these things we need to pay attention to or we will find ourselves back in the labyrinth of the psychopath once more. We have a real responsibility to ourselves and the people around us to not only transcend this experience but become more aware, more wise and more willing to stand up and defend other victims of psychopaths and to explain to all whom we know personally what a psychopath really is and how they function within all levels of society.

We all have one defence mechanism which — even when we are completely lost in the deepest depths of the labyrinth — was available to us all along. It may have been the faintest sensation fluttering deep inside us trying to get our attention, but we more than likely ignored its warnings.

INTUITION WORKS

This lack of understanding, or under-utilising, your own sense of feeling or inner knowing in relation to situations, people, places and things during your lifetime on this planet is the underlying reason why City Hall 'won' or 'shit happened,' and very often why people remain caught within the clutches of a psychopathic control grid longer than they should have. It was how the psychopath held you in their grip for so long. The *thinking* part of you went along in a zombiefied, manipulated state, while the *feeling* part of you was suppressed. Turns out that the feeling part of you was trying to help you all along. It knows everything. It saw the future. It tried to warn you in advance. It was your higher self talking to you, but you were not listening. Your intuition never lies to you, but it takes some practice to begin trusting it again.

Our educational systems, media and even our loved ones often unconsciously, but very often consciously too, condition us to react to events and situations confronting us in ways which contradict our gut feeling at the time. In a thousand different ways, they stress the importance of *thinking* the thoughts they have implanted in us and denigrate and ridicule *feeling*. This is because the rules on which society is based are there to keep the psychopathic control grid working. Intuition can be our insurance policy to keep us safe from manipulation and mind control.

RESTORATION

Most of the books and research work dealing with the issue of recovery from a psychopath is to get away, leave them and never contact them ever again. This is excellent advice, but it is not going to deal with the main damage the psychopath has done to you emotionally and spiritually. The only way to overcome this is to regain the energy they stole from you.

Hating them is no good. In fact, it is completely counterproductive as they feed off your hate. To them it is just energy they can suck from your being, just like the love energy they robbed from you. They are driven by the quest for our emotional, sexual, social, material and spiritual energy. This applies equally to being a victim of a psychopathic organisations, corporations or regimes. As above, so below — macrocosm and microcosm.

Do not feed the beast with anger and fear. That's what the psychopathic control grid desires from you the most as it justifies their further control and oppression. Hate sends you right back into the darkest corners of the labyrinth.

YOU CAN NEVER OUT-PSYCHOPATH A PSYCHOPATH.

They have had a lifetime of destroying others and manipulating the human condition for their own aim, so forget about 'taking them on one-on-one,' forget about 'fighting fire with fire' — they will simply destroy you. More importantly, they will do it with a song in their heart. You are the only one who is entirely emotionally invested in this 'war' with the psychopath, but you'll ultimately be nothing more than a peashooter firing at an Apache gunship. You will lose and it might even kill you — either through physical violence at the hands of the psychopath, or the destruction of your personal and professional reputation, or their hiring a hit man to kill you, or you'll give yourself cancer from the torment and misery.

The *I Ching* states that we should *"Never confront evil directly. Never call it evil directly because evil always finds weapons to defend itself."*

When it comes to dealing with psychopaths, the I Ching is correct. Your task is not vengeance, but caring for and about yourself on the road to full mental, spiritual and physical health. Walk away and leave the psychopath to eventually render themselves socially obsolete and without enablers. It always ends up the same for them. Always.

Tragically, many people in relationships with psychopaths, finding themselves suddenly discarded and devalued, can literally die.

Japanese cardiologists discovered a phenomenon called 'stress cardiomyopathy,' when an intense emotional situation arises, such as the loss of a loved one, causes dysfunction in the ventricular chamber resulting in heart failure in people without previous signs of heart disease. The heart muscle temporarily weakens, causing it to literally break. This situation, now referred to as 'broken heart syndrome,' is caused by deep emotional stress — exactly the state most people coming out of a relationship with a psychopath experience.

This is a very serious public health issue, as researchers at Johns Hopkins University discovered. Women who had this syndrome often succumb to heart failure, though they had none of the usual predisposing factors of heart disease. What had initiated the condition was purely psychological, due to the sudden divorce or the death of a loved one.

We may never know how many men and women have died of heart failure having been instantly devalued and discarded by a psychopath. This is why victims must begin to take care of their health with extreme urgency. It can literally be a life or death matter, and you dying would delight the psychopath no end — especially if they have an insurance policy on you. Psychopaths are not real humans, just in case you haven't figured this out by now. They are dangerous hominid predators.

Carefully studying your personality and traits, coupled with calling on their incredible internal radar for potential victims is how psychopaths locate their prey, how the psychopaths extract/feed from their victims energy, and more disturbingly how the psychopath keeps a hold on the victims even for many years afterward they have left. Matters not if the psychopath is on the other side of the world, they still have a hoard of your life energy, soul, call it what you will, inside their bodies.

Psychopaths have an uncanny ability to literally drain people of their emotional energy. Look at it this way: if you are in an enclosed room and the fire is on, you are comfortable and warm. Suddenly, someone opens the door, the heat instantly leaves the room and you are hit with the draught and cold. This is where the wind in our weather comes from; cold and hot air interacting. Now apply this to psychopaths. We are emotionally warm inside. They are emotionally cold inside. If there is duality of everything in nature then this can be applied to our emotional energies as well.

Through my research I have discovered we can take this living energy back, we reclaim what we have invested in the psychopath's body. I came upon this method by a chance encounter with a member of a meditation support group in the UK who successfully uses personal intention and visualisation to help female victims of rape get back their emotional energy from the rapists who took it from them.

All I did was adapt this system for my own personal use to deal with psychopaths from my own past. Let's be honest; coming out of a relationship with a psychopath is just like being in a kind of rape experience. You were just raped tip-toe style over a number of months and years rather than in one vicious attack.

How does this technique work? Honestly, I have no idea and this is for others to speculate. But I do know for a fact this does work and others I have suggested this to have told me the same. You will feel so much better the more you do it. Studies on meditation reveal that the power of our thoughts affects reality. If this is the case, what could happen if we all started focusing on what we want instead of what we don't want or are afraid of? Quantum Physics tells us everything is energy — so why not learn to take back this energy which the psychopaths have sadistically harvested from us.

How to Remove your Energy from a Psychopath who Stole it

Find a dark, quiet, comfortable room with no interruptions

Relax and pay attention to your heartbeat

Imagine that your life force is a twinkling sparklingly coloured light or radiant mist

Now think of some of your light force trapped inside the DNA of the psychopath who stole it from you

Imagine this light leaving their body as a ball and travelling back from any distance, back into your own living energy

That's it. You will not believe how much better you feel almost instantly. Keep doing this technique whenever you find yourself having a bad moment thinking about what the psychopath did to you. In most cases of psychopathic behaviour the quest for the emotional energy from others is usually subconscious while they are manipulating and robbing us. In the same way normal people are not really conscious that we are absorbing Vitamin C when we eat an orange, the psychopath is sucking the energy out of their victims as a matter of course. This is why sexual promiscuity is vital to the psychopath as the release of emotional energy in the victim is so valuable to them.

Being a victim of a psychopath is a unique experience almost none of us has been trained in, educated in or even remotely informed on how to deal with. In many ways the victims, if unable to recover from the experience, can be become a sort of un-people within society. They carry this pain and deep sorrow inside them and yet they find it so hard to express the intensity of the anguish.

How can one express that split second in the morning when you first wake up, and or a brief moment you are perfectly normal, then the memory of the psychopath enters your mind and a wave of toxic floodwaters races through your body. You dig your fingers into the pillow and start shaking and can't believe what is happening to you.

"Where has the real me gone?" You will ask yourself this question time and time again. It is almost as if in the aftermath of a psychopathic relationship the victims have to spend part of the recovery period moving around looking for the fragments of their broken souls — finding a piece now and again in the hope they can be themselves once more.

For most victims, the turning point is finally realising that you were not dealing with a human being and as a result you are under no obligation to furnish any psychopath with the courtesy, respect and decency human beings deserve.

When you eventually understand that it is the psychopaths themselves who are the living dead, and that they are little more than mobile cadavers in search of the energy of others, that's when we start to become reborn. It's not about hating them after a while, it's about recognising them for what they are. Then everything changes.

Psychopaths, in the emotional and spiritual sense, are no more alive than a shop window mannequin that is capable of movement and speech. When the realisation finally dawns on you that this is how they really are and why they were drawn to you in the first place, then the real you returns.

Take your energy back from them. No Contact Ever Again stops the flow of energy to the psychopath and then the energy retrieval method outlined above brings it back to you. Then you have fully recovered and the heavy steel door to the labyrinth of the psychopath slams shut for all eternity. The psychopath is trapped behind it forever and you walk to freedom a wiser and more mature person with a fully restored psychological, emotional and spiritual wellness.

PSYCHOPATHS KNOW EXACTLY WHAT THEY ARE DOING

How many times have you been in their company and watched their wild, frantic eyes racing from side to side, their quick nodding of self-satisfaction and the shifty little smile which rises on the corner of their mouth. This is perhaps the only time we ever get to see their real homo-feral 'emotions'. If you can call them emotions. More like auto-sadistic impulses.

Do not listen to people who tell you psychopaths are innocent victims of genetics, poor homes or biochemical imbalances. Factors such as their wacky brain electrical system and high testosterone levels are considered glorious attributes enjoyed by the psychopath. I have spent years looking into every aspect of the psychopath and I am now completely convinced, beyond a shadow of a doubt, that psychopaths are not human beings as we understand human beings to be — they are not 'us'. Not even close.

As soon as you get wise to their scams, the on-tap crocodile tears, the gaslighting, the devaluing, the word salad, the mimicry, the lies, the inconsistencies, the cruelty, the selective memory and — if all that fails — the arrogant indignation, you will be able to say and mean it, *"They are so predictable."*

At this point, seeing a psychopath 'in the wild' becomes a zoological exercise in which you are ideally suited to observe and educate others in spotting and avoiding this other, alien entity.

As a final note, never turn to abusing alcohol, drugs or other addictive substances following your survival of a psychopath. You are bigger than that, and the rest of us love and need you just the way you are.

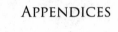

APPENDICES

Early European woodcut portraying a woman
who is compelled by her inner demon to use
her vanity and charm to seduce and steal
gold from men.

TRANSSOCIOPATHICA
PSYCHOPATHS IN FOLKLORE

This book has been the culmination of a journey which began in 2008 when I decided to write a fictional novel/screenplay based on psychopaths being a product of demonic possession. When I created the Transsociopathica website I was developing ideas for story and character development in the hope of gauging how people would react to the overall concept. I was literally stunned by the response and the amount of hits the website received. This would become the genesis of this book. Fiction became fact — fact became fiction.

The concept of a psychopath being a demon that possessed humans really touches something deep within the human psyche at a very intense level. Be it a result of a collective folk memory, or if indeed we are prone to indulge this concept as part of the healing process, the reality is like everything in nature it exists for a reason, including normal people convinced they have encountered a demon in the guise of the psychopath who came into their life.

The psychopath or sociopath has been represented throughout history, either as metaphor or allegory in the guise of the demon, the djinn, the succubus, the vampire, and the werewolf. Even in the twenty-first century this instinctual response is as strong as ever after someone has encountered the full absurdity and horror presented by the pathology.

Another historical woodcut showing an individual
who journeys from town to town compelled by
their inner demon to seek people to befriend
in order to steal their belongings.

What I found truly amusing about the Transsociopathica site was the comments left by self-professed 'intellectuals' and other hilariously self-righteous types who could not recognise that the site was not completely serious. I recall one sanctimonious type accusing me of 'crazy rationalisations'. Most people who visited the site knew that the demonic aspect was just a lure to get people in the door so I could get their feedback and exchange ideas. However, it never ceased to amaze me that the ones who considered themselves 'scientific' and 'rational' were the last to figure out what was really going on. No doubt most of these types would also be eager transhumanists looking to upgrade those they deem imperfect and failing to measure up to their own elevated self-image.

In the pre-scientific age, the need to diagnose and define the heartless behaviour of individuals and groups was just as strong then as it is now. The average person could not understand what they were being exposed to, what was the cause and the cure for this evil in their midst. These people lived up-close-and-personal with real life 'devils' to a far more visceral and intense degree than many of us do now.

While working in Italy, I took some time off to visit the stately homes and mansions of the Italian nobles, mainly to view their collections of paintings and tapestries housed within often morbid and sinister palaces. I began to notice that many of these homes contained large paintings on wooden panels squared off on three sides with a curved bevelled top. These paintings nearly always contained graphic scenes of battles and other horrors such as executions and murderous retribution of one type or another. I asked a tour guide why these paintings were this strange shape and he explained to me that they were designed to be headboards of matrimonial beds for newly-wed aristocratic couples, given as wedding presents from other nobles. They conceived their children beneath these graphic depictions of the execution of prisoners captured at a battle in Umbria or scenes of an outbreak of plague among the peasantry of Lombardy.

Woman being seduced by a devil in the guise
of a handsome, well-dressed and charming man.
Woodcut, Von den Vnholden und Hexen. (1489)

Is it any wonder that the ordinary Italians in the early Renaissance period who lived under the yoke of these psychopath elites would rationalise their masters as being demons and devils?

There is currently a wealthy and powerful family in the United Arab Emirates who to this day boast of being the bloodline of a demon-human hybrid due to their ancestors mating with female *djinns*. The UAE is one of the wealthiest countries in the world due to its vast oil reserves, yet in 2010 it was reported that nearly one-fifth of the child population of that country is dying of starvation.

Bearing all this in mind, I suspect these "crazy rationalisations" will remain with us for some time to come.

Plus ça change, plus c'est la même chose.

The Psychopath's Heartfelt Farewell

The purpose of these two examples of somewhat satirical text below is to demonstrate the incredible lack of understanding psychopaths have for the emotional impact their behaviour has on normal human beings, coupled with their inability to convincingly fake emotion when they are in 'new target mode' and are grooming their next enabler.

These emails are composites based on real emails, phone texts, and letters written to partners, spouses and families abandoned with no prior warning. The examples below will give the reader more of an insight into the psychopathic mind than five years studying for a PhD in Psychology.

> Dear Jane,
>
> Since finding out you have multiple sclerosis I cannot stand to remain with you and see you suffer. It is killing me more than you.
>
> I have left you for a woman in Birmingham I just met on a widows' message board last night. We are deeply in love. I am nearly 60 now and Jett's last chance to be a rock star is fading. It is now or never. There is no money left in our joint account as I needed it for the plane ticket and my first guitar lesson. I know you understand. Can we get divorced very soon as I need to remarry ASAP as I need a place to store my collection of guitars and amps.
>
> You are one special lady. It would break Jett's heart if I never heard from you again. I did not tell you this to your face as I did not want to upset you. As I know how much you love me and support me.
>
> Eternal Love Until the Last Encore at the End of the Gig!
>
> Jett—Rock On XXX

Dear John,

I had a long think about our five years and two kids together and things are not OK. I did not reply to your emails and phone calls during the last 48 hours as I was so deeply devastated about us and what has happened.

I have left you for a man in New Jersey I met on Facebook last week. We are deeply in love. Unlike you, he is there for me constantly and is not working endless hours to pay for a nanny and housekeeper. We both like *Family Guy* a lot too! Can we get divorced very soon as I need to remarry ASAP.

You are a special guy and I'll always be your 'Stacy Shortcake'. I know how much you and the kids love me—but you would have no right to shout at me as this is all your fault. You worry too much John and you need to relax and enjoy life more dummy! Oh and this morning while packing my bags I finally got around to watching the *Family Guy* DVD box set! Was soooooooooooo funny. Such a great show. Stewie is so kewl lol!

Love

Stacy Shortcake! XXXXX

PS: That other email which arrived in your in-box addressed to another guy's name with the title 'SWEETER TASTING SPERM' was not sent by me. A woman also called Stacy and who also uses the nickname 'Stacy Shortcake' broke into the house, logged on to my laptop and sent it. Can you believe some people!

Further Reading and Viewing

Snakes in Suits: When Psychopaths Go to Work
Paul Babiak and Robert Hare
HarperBusiness ISBN-10: 0060837721

Without Conscience:
The Disturbing World of the Psychopaths Among Us
Robert D. Hare PhD
The Guilford Press ISBN-10: 1572304510

The Sociopath Next Door
Martha Stout
Broadway. ISBN-10: 0767915828

A Dance With the Devil:
A True Story of Marriage to a Psychopath
Barbara Bentley
Berkley Trade. ISBN-10: 0425221180

The Myth of Sanity:
Divided Consciousness and the Promise of Awareness
Martha Stout
Penguin (Non-Classics) ISBN-10: 0142000558

The Corporation:
The Pathological Pursuit of Profit and Power
Joel Bakan
Free Press ISBN-10: 0743247442

The Search for the "Manchurian Candidate":
The CIA and Mind Control:
The Secret History of the Behavioral Sciences
John D. Marks
W. W. Norton & Company ISBN-10: 0393307948

Political Ponerology:
A Science on the Nature of Evil Adjusted for Political Purposes
Andrew M. Lobaczewski
Red Pill Press ISBN-10: 1897244479

RECOMMENDED RECOVERY WEBSITES

Narcissistic Sociopath (Survivor Support Group) on Facebook
http://www.facebook.com/

LoveFraud
http://www.lovefraud.com/

Men Who Are Abused
http://menwhoareabused.com/

Thomas Sheridan on YouTube
http://www.youtube.com/user/ThomasSheridanArts

RECOMMENDED SITES WITH INFORMATION ON PSYCHOPATHS AND PSYCHOPATHIC BEHAVIOUR

Robert Hare's website devoted to the study of Psychopathy
http://www.hare.org/

The Path Whisperer
http://pathwhisperer.wordpress.com/

FURTHER VIEWING

Michael Tsarion's Architects of Control
http://architectsofcontrol.com/

A HANDY PHRASEBOOK:

WHEN A PSYCHOPATH SAYS,
"I LOVE YOU UNTIL THE END OF THE WORLD."
Translation: "You'll do for now."

WHEN A PSYCHOPATH SAYS,
"I AM SO SORRY TO HEAR ABOUT THE DEATH OF YOUR FATHER."
Translation: "Don't spend too long mourning as I'll get bored and find someone else more fun."

WHEN A PSYCHOPATH SAYS,
"YOU'RE CONFUSING THE ISSUE."
Translation: "Keep explaining, I've run out of ammo to hit you with."

WHEN A PSYCHOPATH SAYS:
"NEVER MIND ME—LET'S TALK ABOUT YOU."
Translation: "No way am I telling you about the other idiots I have screwed over before we met."

WHEN A PSYCHOPATH SAYS:
"I CAN'T TAKE THIS ANYMORE."
Translation: "Now beg me to come back."

WHEN A PSYCHOPATH SAYS:
"NO INCOME TAX INCREASES."
Translation: "We'll hide it as a public service charge."

WHEN A PSYCHOPATH SAYS:
"THIS IS MY FAMILY."
Translation: "I own them."

WHEN A PSYCHOPATH SAYS:
"YOU REALLY DRIVE ME MAD."
Translation: "Don't make me hit you. I'll hurt my hand."

WHEN A PSYCHOPATH SAYS:
"WE CAN STILL BE FRIENDS"
Translation: "I am using a screwdriver right now, but you are the best hammer I ever had, so stay on the shelf where I can get to you if I need you for something the screwdriver cannot do."

WHEN A PSYCHOPATH SAYS:
"THANK YOU."
Translation: "Next time, bring it sooner."

WHEN A PSYCHOPATH SAYS:
"I LOVE YOU UNCONDITIONALLY."
Translation: "I heard that on TV."

WHEN A PSYCHOPATH SAYS:
"YOU ARE THE ONE I HAVE BEEN SEARCHING FOR MY ENTIRE LIFE."
Translation: "I'm lining you up as my next victim."

WHEN A PSYCHOPATH SAYS:
"NO ONE KNOWS YOU LIKE I DO."
Translation: "Because you're going to be exactly what I want you to be."

WHEN A PSYCHOPATH SAYS:
"I LOVE HEARING YOU TALK ABOUT YOURSELF, YOUR LIFE, YOUR HOPES AND DREAMS AND FEARS."
Translation: "Don't mind the recording device in my pocket. I like to make transcripts for future reference."

WHEN A PSYCHOPATH SAYS:
"YOU NEED ME."
Translation:" I want you to feel so completely dependent and incompetent you have to ask my permission to take your next breath."

WHEN A PSYCHOPATH SAYS:
"I BELIEVE IN FREEDOM."
Translation: "Mine, not yours.

A PSYCHOPATH SAYS:
"WHAT DO YOU LIKE ABOUT ME?"
Translation: "Give me an ego-hit, I'm running low."

WHEN A PSYCHOPATH SAYS:
"WHO TAKES BETTER CARE OF YOU THAN I DO?"
Translation: "You know you can't take care of yourself."

WHEN A PSYCHOPATH SAYS:
"HE MADE THE BIG TIME ALRIGHT, BUT HE WOULD HAVE
BEEN NOTHING WITHOUT ME GUIDING HIM IN THE EARLY
DAYS."
Translation: "I made fun of him when he bought his first drum kit."

WHEN A PSYCHOPATH SAYS:
"YOU KNOW THAT'S NOT WHAT I MEANT SO STOP TWIST-
ING MY WORDS."
Translation: "Twisting words is MY thing!"

WHEN A PSYCHOPATH SAYS:
"YOU KNOW WHAT I MEAN?"
*Translation: "I can't think of anything to brainwash you with right now. It's
more fun to watch you figure out how to make me happy. Sort of like watching a gerbil running on a wheel. Or maybe an aquarium. Relaxing, y'know?"*

WHEN A PSYCHOPATH SAYS:
"I CAN SEE SOMETHING VERY SPECIAL IN YOU..."
Translation: "...that I can totally exploit for my own needs."

WHEN A PSYCHOPATH SAYS:
"WHERE DID THE SWEET, FUN-LOVING PERSON I MARRIED
GO?"
Translation: "I'm bored."

WHEN A PSYCHOPATH SAYS:
"YOU NEED TO TAKE RESPONSIBILITY FOR THE FAILURE OF
THIS RELATIONSHIP."
Translation: 'Because I sure as hell won't."

WHEN A PSYCHOPATH SAYS:
"YOU ARE THE MOST BEAUTIFUL WOMAN IN THE WORLD,
INSIDE AND OUT."
Translation: "And every last one of you fall for that line every single time."

WHEN A PSYCHOPATH SAYS:
"SIX WEEKS AGO YOU WERE THE SWEETEST AND MOST
WONDERFUL PERSON I EVER MET. NOW I HAVE MY
DOUBTS."
Translation: "You used to be so gullible."

WHEN A PSYCHOPATH SAYS:
"THEY ALL STABBED ME IN THE BACK."
Translation: "They figured me out."

WHEN A PSYCHOPATH SAYS:
"YOU ARE SO SECURE AND SELF-CONFIDENT. I AM REALLY
ATTRACTED TO THAT ASPECT OF YOU."
*Translation: "It is my single-minded mission to make you doubt yourself. For
the rest of your life."*

WHEN A PSYCHOPATH SAYS:
"PLEASE TALK TO ME."
Translation: "I think your brainwashing may be wearing off."

WHEN A PSYCHOPATH SAYS:
"YOU DROVE ME AWAY."
Translation: "You figured me out."

WHEN A PSYCHOPATH SAYS:
"OH GOD, PLEASE DON'T DO ANYTHING HORRIBLE LIKE
COMMIT SUICIDE!"
Translation: "Everybody will blame me."

WHEN A PSYCHOPATH SAYS:
"WE ARE IMPLEMENTING THESE NEW SECURITY MEASURES
TO PROTECT CITIZENS FROM TERRORISTS WHO THREATEN
YOUR LIBERTY AND FREEDOM."
*Translation: "Your four year-old daughter is wearing My Little Pony under-
wear and your nine year-old son has a birthmark on his left buttock."*

WHEN A PSYCHOPATH SAYS:
"I LOVE MY MOTHER MORE THAN ANYONE ON EARTH."
Translation: "Because she excuses everything I do."

WHEN A PSYCHOPATH SAYS:
"I DID IT TO PROTECT YOU."
Translation: "I did it to protect me."

WHEN A PSYCHOPATH SAYS:
"I'VE NEVER HAD THIS PROBLEM BEFORE WITH ANYONE."
Translation: "I always have this problem with everyone eventually."

WHEN A PSYCHOPATH SAYS:
"WE ARE DIFFERENT PEOPLE NOW THAN WHEN WE MET."
Translation: "I have custom-built a new persona and am ready to implement it any minute now. Bye."

WHEN A PSYCHOPATH SAYS:
"YOU ARE JUST SO DIFFICULT TO BE AROUND."
Translation: "You may be waking from your mind-controlled trance."

WHEN A PSYCHOPATH SAYS:
"ANYONE WHO CLAIMS THAT THE CEOs OF TOP CORPORA-
TIONS, INVESTMENT BANKS, MEMBERS OF THE COUNCIL
ON FOREIGN RELATIONS, THE BILDERBURG GROUP AND
THE UNITED NATIONS ARE INVOLVED IN DEVELOPING A
NON-DEMOCRATIC ONE WORLD GOVERNMENT FOR THE
BENEFIT OF AN ELITE MINORITY, THEY ARE INSANE CON-
SPIRACY THEORISTS SUFFERING FROM DELUSIONS AND
PARANOIA!"
Translation: "Go back to watching X-Factor and shut up."

EXIT STRATEGY FROM PSYCHOPATHIC SPOUSE

DIVORCE/ FREEDOM

SECRET DECISION TO EXIT

BEGIN SETTING ASIDE CASH

DOCUMENT ALL PATHOLOGICAL BEHAVIOUR BY SPOUSE

CONFIDE IN SOMEONE CLOSE TO YOU OF THE NATURE OF YOUR PSYCHOPATHIC SPOUSE

DEVELOP EXTERIOR SUPPORT NETWORK/ LIVING ARRANGEMENTS

REINFORCE YOUR LOVE FOR YOUR CHILDREN AND BOND DEEPLY WITH THEM

EXIT HOME

CHILDREN WILL FOLLOW IN TIME

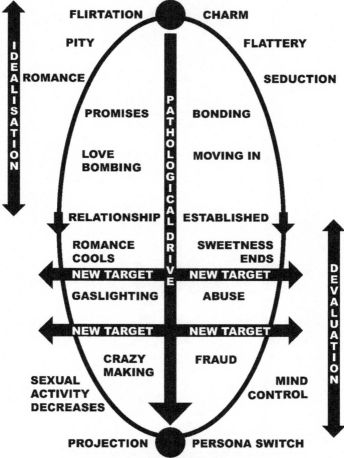

FROM DESIRE TO DISCARD
PSYCHOPATH IDENTIFIES YOU
AS A TARGET

FLIRTATION   CHARM

PITY   FLATTERY

ROMANCE   SEDUCTION

IDEALISATION

PROMISES   BONDING

LOVE BOMBING   MOVING IN

PATHOLOGICAL DRIVE

RELATIONSHIP   ESTABLISHED

ROMANCE COOLS   SWEETNESS ENDS

NEW TARGET   NEW TARGET

GASLIGHTING   ABUSE

NEW TARGET   NEW TARGET

DEVALUATION

CRAZY MAKING   FRAUD

SEXUAL ACTIVITY DECREASES   MIND CONTROL

PROJECTION   PERSONA SWITCH

PSYCHOPATH DISCARDS YOU
FOR NEW TARGET(S)

ABOUT THE AUTHOR

Raised in Dublin, Ireland, Thomas Sheridan is a professional artist currently living and working in south Sligo under the shadow of the Ox Mountains. After moving to New York in the mid 1980s, he became a rock musician playing with the influential Lower East Side goth/post-punk three piece *The Children's Zoo*. Upon leaving the music business in the early 1990s, Thomas studied as a graphic designer and went on to enjoy a successful communications career with several Wall Street investment banks.

Returning to Ireland to pursue his painting career in 1998, he began to write poetry, satirical essays, short stories and socio-political commentaries on subjects ranging from Irish politicians, to psychology, to media manipulation and the occult. These have been published in journals and books worldwide.

Thomas Sheridan's paintings have been described as vibrant, contemplative, poetic and soulful, with an underlying surrealist/symbolist nature. His inspiration is drawn from many sources, from the human condition within the real and emotional landscape, to the nature of reality and relationships. Thomas' work is in private collections worldwide and he has been represented by several galleries. He has also taken part in exhibitions in Ireland and abroad.

"My music, art and writing have been a life-long attempt to create a dialogue with the society and world around me and as a result, to implement a more meaningful dialogue with myself."

www.thomassheridanartist.blogspot.com

ACKNOWLEDGMENTS

I would like to thank the following people for their help and inspiration.

Firstly, everyone who contacted me through my YouTube channel requesting that I write this book after they had watched my *Labyrinth of the Psychopath* video playlist. Your messages of thanks and encouragement were so moving to me. I would also like to thank Raam Barros at Substitution Press (UK) for his initial support and enthusiasm. Thanks to Holly Ollivander of Velluminous Press for helping me lose my author/editor virginity and being so gentle with me, and for her encouragement and belief in this project. Thanks also to my family and friends who have supported me over the years and to the many people who emailed me after stumbling upon my work on everyday psychopaths and graciously offered their own stories and testimonies. Profound gratitude to Diana Schwartz for an exacting proofread for the last revision. Special thanks also goes out to Linda Bennett (Australia), Lourdes Rivera (USA), Alison Gunson (UK) and many others who prefer to remain unnamed. Thank you regardless.

Finally, thank you to all the psychopaths who passed through my life — especially the ones I worked alongside during my time on Wall Street. The notes I took on your behaviour and the conversations I had with you during those years were a valuable insight, though those insights took years to become beneficial lessons in the grand scheme of things. All of you have played an invaluable part in helping to realise this book.

Index

T

CPSIA information can be obtained at www.ICGtesting.com
Printed in the USA
BVOW08s1928060316

439302BV00001B/1/P